P9-AQF-944

Once again, Goodyear Eagles
sweep Indy 500.
First place, second place, third place.

Kenny Brack wins fifth
Indy 500 title for A.J. Foyt.

For the second year in a row, Goodyear swept
the competition with a stunning one, two, three
finish at the Indianapolis 500. Goodyear Racing
Eagles also took four-time Indy winner A.J. Foyt back to
the winner's circle. This time as team owner. Foyt entered
three cars in this year's 33-car field. And all three of A.J.'s
entries finished in the top six. Kenny Brack took the checkered
flag, winning his first Indy 500. Billy Boat finished third. And
Robbie Buhl finished sixth. And all of A.J.'s Dallara/Oldsmobile
Auroras took to the Brickyard on Goodyear Eagle racing
radials. Congratulations to Kenny Brack, Billy Boat,
Robbie Buhl and to second place finisher Jeff Ward
in his Pagan Racing Dallara/Oldsmobile Aurora.
To A.J. Foyt we offer special congratulations. It's
good to have you back home again in Indianapolis.
Back home in the winner's circle.

  MORE VICTORIES. MORE PLACES. MORE OFTEN.

GOODYEAR
#1 in Racing. #1 in Tires.

©1999, The Goodyear Tire & Rubber Company. All rights reserved.

BRICKYARD 400

1999 ANNUAL

OFFICIAL PUBLICATION OF
THE INDIANAPOLIS MOTOR SPEEDWAY

AL PEARCE

MBI Publishing Company

Just 14 guys working furiously to remain anonymous.

Guys on the Pennzoil Pit Crew aren't asked to sign many autographs and their faces don't adorn cereal boxes.

Yet without their expertise, racing wouldn't be the most exciting team sport in the world. Stop. Go.

PENNZOIL

©1999 Pennzoil - Quaker State Company.

Contents

Practice Sessions By Al Pearce   9

Official Entry List   16

First-Round Qualifying   18
Gordon's Cool Track Run Stands By Al Pearce

First-Round Qualifying Results   24

Second-Round Qualifying   26
Musgrave's 176.943 mph is the Best of the Rest By Al Pearce

Second-Round Qualifying Results   30

Starting Line-Up   31

Open-Wheel Wizards   33
Gordon and Stewart Lead the Charge Into NASCAR's Upper Echelon By Dave Argabright

The 1999 Brickyard 400   53
D.J. Delivers By Al Pearce

Official Box Score   81

Driver Positions By 10-Lap Intervals   82

Driver Profiles By Al Pearce   84

First published in 1999 by MBI Publishing Company, 729 Prospect Avenue, PO Box 1, Osceola, WI 54020-0001 USA

© IMS Corporation, 1999
All rights reserved. With the exception of quoting brief passages for the purposes of review, no part of this book may be reproduced without prior written permission from the Publisher.

The information in this book is true and complete to the best of our knowledge. All recommendations are made without any guarantee on the part of the author or Publisher, who also disclaim any liability incurred in connection with the use of this data or specific details.

We recognize that some works, model names and designations, for example, mentioned herein are the property of the trademark holder. We use them for identification purposes only. This is not an official publication. All photos are from the IMS photo archives.

MBI Publishing Company books are also available at discounts in bulk quantity for industrial or sales-promotional use. For details, write to Special Sales Manager at Motorbooks International Wholesalers & Distributors, 729 Prospect Avenue, PO Box 1, Osceola, WI 54020-0001 USA.

Edited by Lee Klancher • Designed by Rebecca Allen
Printed in Hong Kong ISBN 0-7603-773-3

The 1999 Brickyard 400 may well be remembered as Dale Jarrett making good on his resolve to win again at Indianapolis after a miscalculation cost him a win in 1998. Jarrett became a two-time winner at the Brickyard with a convincing ride to victory before a full house of racing fans.

Fans expect to see the best when they enter the gates of the Indianapolis Motor Speedway, and NASCAR's Winston Cup Series delivered again in the sixth running of one of racing's biggest events. Wonderful weather, enthusiastic fans and great racing combined for three days of motorsports entertainment.

Dale Jarrett shared the spotlight with two others: Dale Earnhardt and Mark Martin. Martin captured his second straight IROC (International Race of Champions) event at the Brickyard, but Earnhardt clinched the IROC series title.

None of the exciting action would have been possible without the hundreds of thousands of fans that crowded the Indianapolis Motor Speedway during three days in August, sharing their enthusiasm for all that racing stands for in this country.

On behalf of the Hulman-George family and all of the employees of the Indianapolis Motor Speedway, I want to extend a sincere thank you for supporting IMS and the events we have. And, I want to invite you back for another exciting season in 2000.

–Tony George

Indianapolis Motor Speedway Corporation

Board of Directors

Mari H. George
Chairman of the Board

Anton H. "Tony" George
President & Chief Executive Officer

M. Josephine George

Nancy L. George

Katherine M. George

Jack R. Snyder

Executive Staff

Jeffrey G. Belskus
Executive Vice President
& Chief Operating Officer

John Newcomb
Vice President,
Sales & Marketing

Leo Mehl
Vice President & Executive
Director of the Pep Boys
Indy Reacing League

W. Curtis Brighton
Vice President &
General Counsel

Fred J. Nation
Vice President, Corporate
Communications &
Public Relations

Peggy Swalls
Vice President,
Administration

Laura George
Staff Advisor

Kenneth T. Ungar
Chief of Staff

Speedway Staff

Don Bailey
Vehicle Coordinator

Dawn Bair
Manager of Creative Services

Ellen Bireley
Manager of Museum Services

Dr. Henry Bock
Director of Medical Services

Martha Briggs
Manager of Accounting

Jeff Chapman
Director of Marketing & Branding

Randy Clark
Manager of Food & Beverage

Sean Clayton
Manager of Market Research

Donald Davidson
Historian

Derek Decker
Manager of Corporate Hospitality

Jeff Dotterer
Applications Manager

Chuck Ferguson
Director of Information Services

Brenda Ferryman
Manager of Mail Services

Kevin Forbes
Director of Engineering & Construction

Lee Gardner
Director of Automotive Partnerships

Lynn Greggs
Director of Accounting & Administration

Mel Harder
Director of Facility Operations

Pat Hayes
Manager of Contract Administration

Marty Hunt
Manager of Track Racing Operations

John Kesler
Manager of Sales

Jeff Kleiber
Manager of Event Operations

Jon Koskey
Technical Manager

Patricia Kuhn
Director of Human Resources

John Lewis
Manager of Facilities

Lisa Lewis
Manager of Human Resources

Kent Liffick
Director of Sponsorship Development

Mai Lindstrom
Director of Public Relations

Bruce Lynch
Director of Retail Sales & Operations

Buddy McAtee
Director of Sales

Matt McCartin
Manager of Promotions

Richard McComb
Director of Finance

Robert McInteer
Director of Safety

Ron McQueeney
Director of Photography

Nancy Miller
Manager of Public Relations

David Moroknek
Director of Licensing &
Consumer Products

Gloria Novotney
Director of Credentials

Dan Petty
Manager of Retail Merchandising

Nicole Polsky
Manager of Licensing

Bruce Ralston
Manager of Telecommunications

Lisa Sommers
Manager of Public Relations,
Special Events

Meeting of the mechanical minds: Smokey Yunick, one of stock car racing's most colorful characters and a master car builder in the sport's formative years, chats with three-time Winston Cup champion crew chief Ray Evernham.

Morning

Labonte, Andretti, Jarrett, and Skinner Top 179

By Al Pearce

Rich Bickle, in the 10-10-345 No. 45 Pontiac, was the first driver out for practice when the weekend's first session opened at 10:00 A.M. Mark Martin, in the No. 6 Valvoline Ford, was next out, followed within the next 71 minutes by 51 more drivers. But it wasn't until 11:39, when Gary Bradberry did a lap in the No. 80 Stan Hover Motorsports Ford, that all 55 drivers had been on the track.

Four of the drivers were credited with being fastest at various stages of the 2-hour session. Bickle led briefly, but only because he was the first through the timing lights. Martin was atop the speed chart for a few moments, then Jeremy Mayfield was there from 10:26 until Bobby Labonte displaced him with 19 minutes left in the session.

When the session ended at 12:28 P.M., Labonte's lap of 179.119 miles per hour was the fastest. John Andretti's 179.044 lap was second-fastest, followed by Dale Jarrett's 179.009, Mike Skinner's 179.005, and the 178.966 of David Green. At other points during the session, Ward Burton, Jeff Gordon, and Sterling Marlin had been among the five fastest.

Three brief caution periods interrupted the session. Safety crews went out early, checking for debris. Moments later, rookie Buckshot Jones pancaked the right side of his No. 00 Crown Fiber Pontiac against the outside wall between Turns 1 and 2. The final caution was at 10:36, when Boris Said's No. 14 Federated Auto Parts Ford blew its engine and quit rolling at the pit road entrance.

Much pre-race attention centered around Tony Stewart, something of a sentimental favorite, thanks to his local ties and the speed he had shown in his Winston Cup rookie season. Stewart's Pontiac was among the dozen quickest cars on Thursday.

The 1995 Brickyard 400 champion Dale Earnhardt marked himself as a contender from the time practice opened on Thursday, keeping his Goodwrench Chevrolet near the top of the time sheets.

Thanks to Dale Jarrett's consistent speeds in the prequalifying practice sessions, the garage area buzz pegged his Ford as the early favorite for the Brickyard 400. Jarrett lived up to the hype.

Afternoon

Irvan's 177+ Stands Tall

By Al Pearce

The day's second practice session began at 4:00 P.M., a half-hour after Pole Qualifying. Speeds were between 4 and 6 miles per hour slower than those at the morning practice, evidence that crews had changed from the morning's qualifying package to their race setup.

Kevin Lepage in the No. 16 TV Guide Ford was first out. Early in the 45-minute session, Ernie Irvan ran 177.644 miles per hour, more than 2 miles per hour faster than his 46th-fastest qualifying lap. He explained that his morning or afternoon speed would have made the top 25 if he'd been able to run either in qualifying. Unfortunately, his qualifying run was spoiled when the Kodak Chevrolet had a problem "The four car ahead of us in line blew up and dumped oil on the track," he said. "It's really not his fault, but the seven cars behind him didn't run like they had in practice."

When the second practice session ended at 4:45 P.M., Irvan's 177.066 lap was still the fastest. Joe Nemechek's 175.953 was second followed by Rich Bickle's 175.635, the 174.581 of Jeff Green, and the 174.466 of Kyle Petty. Fifteen drivers skipped the session: Gordon, Rudd, Sadler, Irwin, Jarrett, Blaney, Mayfield, David Green, Terry Labonte, Boris Said, Ward Burton, Derrike Cope, Dave Marcis, Ricky Craven, and Mike Wallace.

The only incident was a fender-bender between Martin and Rusty Wallace at 4:30, shortly before the session ended. Wallace came rolling out of Gasoline Alley as Martin was accelerating down pit road, near the pit wall opening. The right-front of Wallace's car clipped Martin's driver-side door, but neither suffered major damage and neither driver was injured.

Eyes on the prize. At a Friday photo shoot for past Winston Cup winners at Indianapolis, Jeff Gordon seemed to be contemplating just how a third Brickyard trophy might look on his mantle.

The brothers Labonte—that's Terry on the left, looking a bit amused at Bobby's antics—pass some time together in Gasoline Alley. Bobby was on the pace all weekend, while Terry's team was a tick behind.

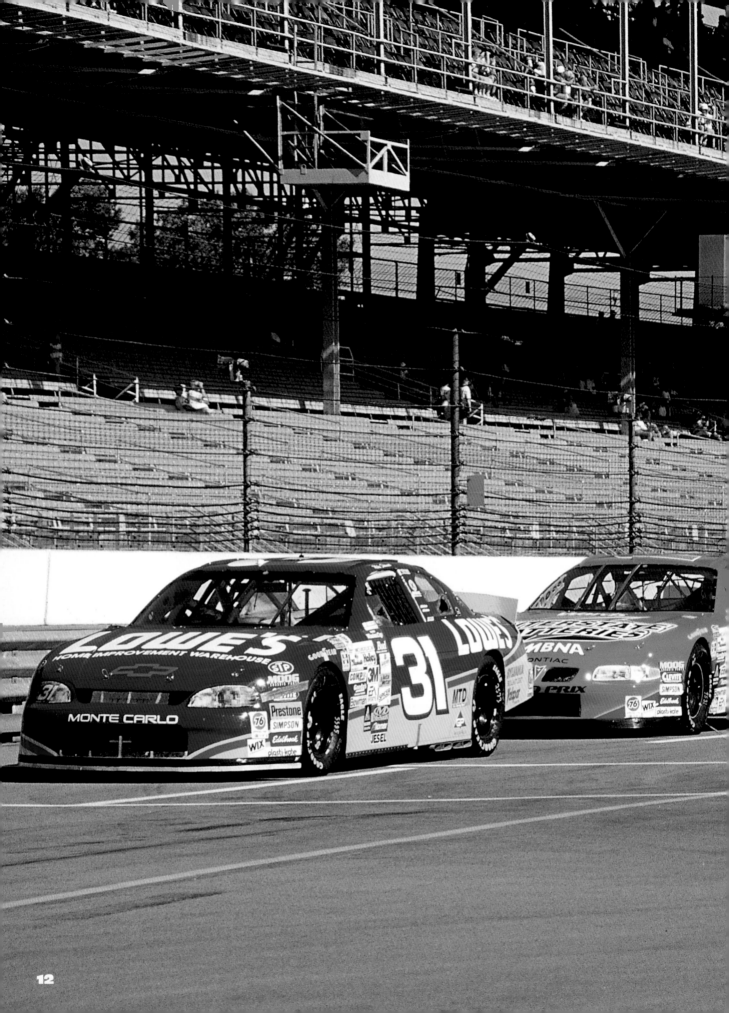

A squadron of Winston Cup cars and drivers await their turns as practice gets under way for the sixth annual Brickyard 400. Given the race's prestige, every warm-up session was critical.

Morning

Park Posts 178
By Al Pearce

One of the toughest decisions during any NASCAR weekend is whether a team not yet qualified should stand on its first-round speed or forfeit it in hopes of improving in the second session. Decide right and you make the show; choose wrong and you don't.

Pole Qualifying on Thursday put the 25 fastest drivers on the grid. That left 30 more drivers in the "stand or requalify" quandary that required a decision after Friday's first practice session. Once the team's representative signed the "Stand On Time" sheet at the Winston Cup office, there was no turning back.

Fourteen teams elected to stand. Some were so certain they couldn't improve that they made their decision shortly after first-round qualifying. Others used Friday's two-hour practice session to gauge whether to stand or requalify. Still other teams—the lucky 25 that had qualified on Thursday—used the practice session to test their cars on long runs in race trim.

Steve Park practiced fastest (178.066 miles per hour), so his Pennzoil team decided to requalify instead of taking a chance by standing on Thursday's 176.744-mile-per-hour lap. Joe Nemechek (SOT), Rich Bickle (requalify), Derrike Cope (SOT), and Ted Musgrave (requalify) joined Park as the session's five fastest under ideal conditions.

One statistic shows that some teams practiced with an eye toward requalifying, while others practiced in race trim: Only four of the session's 20 fastest drivers—Ward Burton, Mark Martin, John Andretti, and Jeff Gordon—were already safely in the 400 field.

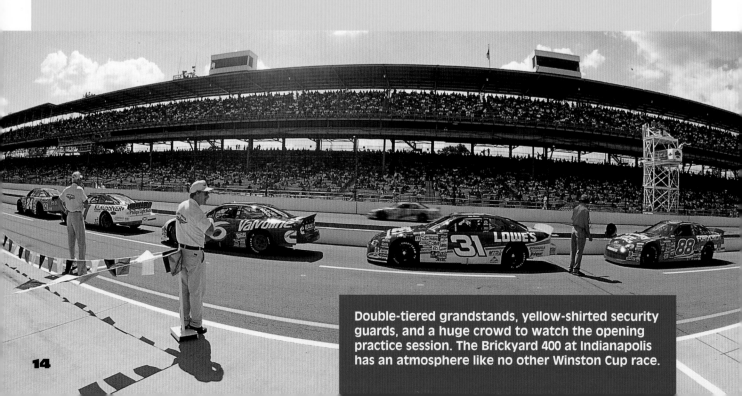

Double-tiered grandstands, yellow-shirted security guards, and a huge crowd to watch the opening practice session. The Brickyard 400 at Indianapolis has an atmosphere like no other Winston Cup race.

Final Practice

Happy Hour at the Brickyard

By Al Pearce

Among racing's many mysteries is the origin of "Happy Hour." Seldom happy and sometimes not an hour, the term is universally accepted to mean the last practice session before the weekend's feature race.

Happy Hour for this year's Brickyard 400 began at 1:49 Friday afternoon. It seemed appropriate that Jeff Gordon, a two-time 400 winner and this year's pole-sitter, was first out. He ran his fastest lap of the session on Lap 3, then settled in for long runs to check his car's fuel mileage and handling characteristics. By the end of the 1-hour session, his best lap of 171.818 stood only eighth-quickest.

Jeremy Mayfield ended the session atop the speed chart. His best lap of 172.957 came during his second lap on the track. Similarly, Dale Jarrett's second-best lap of 172.722 came during his third lap. Bobby Labonte was fifth-quickest at 172.302 in his second lap, and Dale Earnhardt's sixth-quickest at 172.022 came in his third lap. Most drivers began the session on fresh tires, which explains why the fastest speeds took place in the first few laps.

There were only a few exceptions to that "best laps are early laps" pattern: Hut Stricklin's best was his 11th during the session; Joe Nemechek's was his 15th; Ernie Irvan and Ward Burton ran their best laps at 16; Bill Elliott at Lap 23; and Mark Martin at 24. The other 36 drivers who practiced—Rick Mast missed the session because of engine problems—recorded their best laps between their second and ninth laps.

> As if searching out one another's strengths and weaknesses, Dale Earnhardt, Jeff Gordon, and John Andretti did a bit of high-speed jousting during practice.

> Straining for even the slightest glimpse of their favorite cars, NASCAR fans took advantage of the fine summer weather to trade an afternoon of work for an afternoon at the race track.

1999 Entry List

6th Brickyard 400

Indianapolis Motor Speedway • NASCAR Winston Cup Series

Car	Driver/Hometown	Primary Sponsor	Car Make	Team	Owner
1	Steve Park/East Northport, NY	Pennzoil	Chevy Monte Carlo	Dale Earnhardt, Inc.	Dale Earnhardt
2	Rusty Wallace/St. Louis, MO	Miller Lite	Ford Taurus	Penske South Racing	Roger Penske
3W	Dale Earnhardt/Kannapolis, NC	GM Goodwrench	Chevy Monte Carlo	Richard Childress Racing	Richard Childress
4	Bobby Hamilton/Nashville, TN	Kodak Film	Chevy Monte Carlo	Morgan-McClure Motorsports	Larry McClure
5	Terry Labonte/Corpus Christi, TX	Kellogg's	Chevy Monte Carlo	Hendrick Motorsports	Rick Hendrick
6	Mark Martin/Batesville, AR	Valvoline	Ford Taurus	Roush Racing	Jack Roush
7	Michael Waltrip/Owensboro, KY	Philips Electronics	Chevy Monte Carlo	Mattei Motorsports	Jim Mattei
9	Jerry Nadeau/Danbury, CT	Cartoon Network	Ford Taurus	Melling Racing	Mark Melling
10W	Ricky Rudd/Chesapeake, VA	Tide	Ford Taurus	Rudd Performance Motorsports	Linda Rudd
11	Brett Bodine/Chemung, NY	Paychex	Ford Taurus	Brett Bodine Racing	Diane Bodine
12	Jeremy Mayfield/Owensboro, KY	Mobil 1	Ford Taurus	Penske-Kranefuss Racing	Michael Kranefuss
14	Boris Said/Carlsbad, CA	Federated Auto Parts	Ford Taurus	Irvan/Simo	Mark Simo
16	Kevin Lepage/Shelburne, VT	TV Guide	Ford Taurus	Roush Racing	Geoff Smith
18	Bobby Labonte/Corpus Christi, TX	Interstate Batteries	Pontiac Grand Prix	Joe Gibbs Racing	Joe Gibbs
20	Tony Stewart/Rushville, IN	The Home Depot	Pontiac Grand Prix	Joe Gibbs Racing	Joe Gibbs
21	Elliott Sadler/Emporia, VA	CITGO Petroleum Corp.	Ford Taurus	Wood Brothers Racing	Glen Wood
22	Ward Burton/South Boston, VA	Caterpillar	Pontiac Grand Prix	Bill Davis Racing	Bill Davis
23	Jimmy Spencer/Berwick, PA	The Winston	Ford Taurus	Travis Carter Enterprises	Travis Carter
24W	Jeff Gordon/Pittsboro, IN	DuPont	Chevy Monte Carlo	Hendrick Motorsports	Rick Hendrick
25	Wally Dallenbach/Basalt, CO	Budweiser	Chevy Monte Carlo	Joe Hendrick Motorsports	Joe Hendrick
26	Johnny Benson/Grand Rapids, MI	Cheerios	Ford Taurus	Roush Racing	Evan Lyall
28	Kenny Irwin/Indianapolis, IN	Texaco/Havoline	Ford Taurus	Robert Yates Racing	Robert Yates
30	Derrike Cope/Spanaway, WA	Jimmy Dean	Pontiac Grand Prix	Bahari' Racing	Chuck Rider
31	Mike Skinner/Susanville, CA	Lowe's	Chevy Monte Carlo	Richard Childress Racing	Richard Childress
32	Mike Wallace/St. Louis, MO	Ultra Wheels	Ford Taurus	Biagi Brothers	Jim Smith

No.	Driver/Hometown	Sponsor	Make	Team	Owner
33	Ken Schrader/Fenton, MO	Skoal	Chevy Monte Carlo	Andy Petree Racing	Andy Petree
36	Ernie Irvan/Salinas, CA	M & M's	Pontiac Grand Prix	MB2 Motorsports	Tom Beard
40	Sterling Marlin/Columbia, TN	Coors Light	Chevy Monte Carlo	Team SABCO	Felix Sabates
41	David Green/Owensboro, KY	Kodiak	Chevy Monte Carlo	Larry Hedrick Motorsports	Larry Hedrick
42	Joe Nemechek/Lakeland, FL	BellSouth	Chevy Monte Carlo	Team SABCO	Felix Sabates
43	John Andretti/Indianapolis, IN	STP	Pontiac Grand Prix	Petty Enterprises	Richard Petty
44	Kyle Petty/Randleman, NC	Hot Wheels	Pontiac Grand Prix	Petty Enterprises	Kyle Petty
45	Rich Bickle/Edgerton, WI	10-10-345 Lucky Dog Phone Company	Pontiac Grand Prix	Tyler Jet Motorsports	Tim Beverley
50	Ricky Craven/Newburgh, ME	Midwest Transit	Chevy Monte Carlo	Hal Hicks	Hal Hicks
55	Kenny Wallace/St. Louis, MO	Square D	Chevy Monte Carlo	Andy Petree Racing	Andy Petree
58	Hut Stricklin/Calera, AL	Turbine Solutions	Ford Taurus	Scott Barbour	Scott Barbour
60	Geoffrey Bodine/Chemung, NY	PowerTeam	Chevy Monte Carlo	Joe Bessey Motorsports	Joe Bessey
61	Bob Strait/Mokena, IL	Midway Island	Ford Taurus	Mark Thompson	Mark Thompson
62	Jeff Davis/Anaheim Hills, CA	Big Daddy's Bar-B-Que	Ford Taurus	Fenley Motorsports	Randall Fenley
66	Darrell Waltrip/Franklin, TN	Big Kmart/Route 66	Ford Taurus	Haas/Carter Motorsports	Carl Haas
71	Dave Marcis/Wausau, WI	Realtree	Chevy Monte Carlo	Marcis Auto Racing	Helen Marcis
75	Ted Musgrave/Evanston, IL	Remington Arms	Ford Taurus	Butch Mock Motorsports	Butch Mock
77	Robert Pressley/Asheville, NC	Jasper Engines	Ford Taurus	Jasper Motorsports	Doug Bawel
80	Gary Bradberry/Chelsea, AL	Stan Hover Motorsports	Ford Taurus	Stan Hover Motorsports	Stan Hover
88W	Dale Jarrett/Conover, NC	Quality Care Service	Ford Taurus	Robert Yates Racing	Robert Yates
90	Stanton Barrett/Bishop, CA	Donlavey Racing	Ford Taurus	Donlavey Racing	W.C. Donlavey Jr.
91	Dick Trickle/Wisconsin Rapids, WI	All INVINCA-Shield	Chevy Monte Carlo	L.J. Racing	Joe Falk
92	Darrel Krentz/Las Vegas, NV	Race Car Café	Ford Taurus	R.C.D.C. Racing	Eric Zimmerman
93	Dave Blaney/Hartford, OH	Amoco	Pontiac Grand Prix	Bill Davis Racing	Mike Brown
94	Bill Elliott/Dawsonville, GA	McDonald's	Ford Taurus	Bill Elliott Racing	Bill Elliott
97	Chad Little/Spokane, WA	John Deere	Ford Taurus	Roush Racing	Georgetta Roush
98	Rick Mast/Rockbridge Baths, VA	Universal Studios	Ford Taurus	Yarborough Motorsports	Cale Yarborough
99	Jeff Burton/South Boston, VA	Exide Batteries	Ford Taurus	Roush Racing	Bob Corn
00	Buckshot Jones/Monticello, GA	Crown Fiber	Pontiac Grand Prix	Buckshot Racing	Billy R. Jones
01	Jeff Green/Owensboro, KY	TRACFONE	Chevy Monte Carlo	Team SABCO	Carolyn Sabates
05	Morgan Shepherd/Conover, NC	Delco Remy	Pontiac Grand Prix	Cindy J. Shepherd	Cindy J. Shepherd

W = Former Brickyard 400 Winner • Tire: Goodyear • (List Current as of 8/3/99)

FIRST-ROUND QUALIFYING

Gordon's Cool Track Run Stands

By Al Pearce

Jeff Gordon said he was stunned when he won the pole for this year's Brickyard 400. He had an early draw, which meant that he would attempt to qualify just moments after the first of the 55 drivers went out at 1:34 P.M.—during the hottest part of the day (the air temperature was hovering at 81 degrees Fahrenheit and the track temperature was approaching 136 degrees). Generally, drivers whose draw sends them out in such conditions are at a handicap to those who go later.

Gordon had every right to fret. He'd been good, but certainly not exceptional, in the two-hour morning warmup session. His best lap of 178.720 miles per hour was only ninth-fastest, and he had no reason to believe he'd improve significantly when the one-lap qualifying session began early in the afternoon.

With its front-end ducting taped off to reduce aerodynamic drag, Jeff Gordon's Chevrolet jets around the Indianapolis Motor Speedway en route to a new Winston Cup track record of 179.612 miles per hour.

Having set his blistering time early in the qualifying session, Jeff Gordon keeps an eye on the competition with the help of a closed-circuit television monitor in his team's garage. He needn't have worried; no other driver topped the 179 miles-per-hour mark.

As usual at Indianapolis, the pole winner earned a number of additional awards and bonuses. Jeff Gordon needed a few extra pairs of hands to haul his spoils back to Gasoline Alley.

Mike Wallace was the first driver out. He was scheduled to run that night's Craftsman Series truck race at nearby Indianapolis Raceway Park, so NASCAR officials moved him up in line so he wouldn't miss IRP qualifying. Moments after he finished his run, Bill Elliott went out, followed by Dave Marcis. By the time Gordon rolled off pit road, it was 1:44 P.M. and 50,000 pairs of eyes were on him.

He did not disappoint. His 179.612-mile-per-hour lap in the No. 24 DuPont Chevrolet broke Ernie Irvan's year-old stock car track record of 179.394. It was Gordon's 7th pole of the season, the 30th of his brilliant career, and his 3rd (coming after 1995 and 1996) at the Indianapolis Motor Speedway. But he was quick to caution that it was early in the day, and pointed

out that 51 drivers were still in line and all of them had beaten him in practice.

"Give a lot of credit to this team because that wasn't my best lap as a driver," Gordon said well before anything was settled. "The car was tight and I slid the nose, and I didn't hit my marks exactly. The track is hot and slick. Somebody can beat that lap if they catch a cloud. There's a lot of good cars still to go, so I'm not expecting to win the pole. It's good for this time of day, but not for later on."

Mark Martin and crew chief Jimmy Fennig talk shop prior to qualifying. Martin, still smarting from leg and wrist injuries incurred at Daytona in July, admitted to focusing on race set-ups rather than qualifying tricks, but still posted the second-fastest time at Indianapolis.

Below Surprise of the weekend? David Green's third-quickest qualifying time on Thursday afternoon. In the midst of a season fraught with disappointments, the former NASCAR Busch Series champion lit up the Speedway aboard Larry Hedrick's Chevrolet.

Above left Crew chief Larry McReynolds debriefs driver Mike Skinner after Skinner's shot at the time clocks. Always a threat at the fastest Winston Cup tracks, Skinner logged the sixth-best speed on Thursday.

Above Dale Jarrett and crew chief Todd Parrott chat on pit road, no doubt discussing the fickle nature of the Indianapolis Motor Speedway. Though Jarrett was among the heavy favorites for the pole position, a slight bobble in Turn 1 on his flying lap left him outside the second row for the start of the Brickyard 400.

Left The fastest rookie in the Brickyard 400 field was the Hoosier State's own Tony Stewart, who was only too happy to sign a bonus check commemorating his accomplishment. Stewart's qualifying run was good for the 11th starting position.

Opposite Michael Waltrip takes to the track for his qualifying lap—and it was a good one, placing the younger of the racing Waltrip brothers 5th on the grid.

Shows what he knows. Nobody got close, and when all was said and done, Gordon was the only driver to reach the 179-mile-per-hour bracket. Michael Waltrip was briefly second at 178.816, but Mark Martin took that spot for good with a 178.941 lap at 1:58 P.M. Much later, Dale Jarrett bumped Waltrip to third with a lap of 178.859, then David Green shocked everyone with a career-equaling third with a lap of 178.902 miles per hour just 18 minutes before the session ended.

Pole Qualifying established the first 25 starters for the $6.1-million race. Gordon and Martin were on Row 1, Jarrett and Green on Row 2, Waltrip and Mike Skinner on Row 3, Bobby Labonte and Elliott on Row 4, and Ken Schrader and John Andretti on Row 5. The next five rows: Tony Stewart and Ward Burton; Elliott Sadler and Ricky Rudd; Kenny Irwin and Jeff Burton; Rusty Wallace and Dale Earnhardt; and Jeremy Mayfield and Dave Blaney. The last five qualifiers from Round 1 were Sterling Marlin, Terry Labonte, Geoffrey Bodine, Kyle Petty, and Robert Pressley.

Many of NASCAR's most respected drivers didn't come close to the top 25. Three-time champion Darrell Waltrip was 32nd and two-time

Brickyard 400 pole-sitter Ernie Irvan was mired in 46th. Three of Jack Roush's five drivers weren't close to making the field: Kevin Lepage was 42nd, Chad Little was 44th, and Johnny Benson was 47th. Brett Bodine, runner-up to Gordon in the inaugural Brickyard 400, was 43rd, and Bobby Hamilton was 53rd.

After the pole was official, Gordon repeated how stunned he was. "I thought a lot of strong cars—especially those Pontiacs with Bobby Labonte and Ward Burton—would beat us because they were going later, when it would be cooler. Track temperatures make such a big difference here that anybody with a cloud for just a moment will benefit. All in all, I was happy with what I ran even though I thought for sure somebody would beat it."

Martin didn't mince words when asked about Gordon's supposed advantage at IMS. "He's a better driver than at least most of us, if not all of us," he said with his usual candor. "And he drives a better car than most of us, if not all of us. It's a hard combination to beat when you put all that together.

"And I mean that as a compliment in both respects. Not only for the team, but for the driver as well."

First-Round Qualifying Results

6th Brickyard 400

Indianapolis Motor Speedway • NASCAR Winston Cup Series

Chronological Order

Car	Driver	Car Name	Time	Speed	Rank
32	Mike Wallace	Ultra Wheels Ford	51.144	175.974	1
94	Bill Elliott	McDonald's Ford	50.407	178.547	1
71	Dave Marcis	Realtree Chevy	50.825	177.078	2
24	Jeff Gordon	DuPont Automotive Finishes Chevy	50.108	179.612*	1
00	Buckshot Jones	Crown Fiber Pontiac	51.612	174.378	5
98	Rick Mast	Team Woody Ford	51.094	176.146	4
60	Geoffrey Bodine	PowerTeam Chevy	50.668	177.627	3
91	Dick Trickle	All INVINCA-Shield Chevy	51.069	176.232	5
16	Kevin LePage	TV Guide Ford	51.290	175.473	8
7	Michael Waltrip	Philips Electronics Chevy	50.331	178.816	2
6	Mark Martin	Valvoline Ford	50.296	178.941	2
2	Rusty Wallace	Miller Lite Ford	50.566	177.985	5
12	Jeremy Mayfield	Mobil 1 Ford	50.583	177.925	6
33	Ken Schrader	Skoal Chevy	50.415	178.518	5
40	Sterling Marlin	Coors Light Chevy	50.661	177.651	8
58	Hut Stricklin	MTX Audio/CT Farms Ford	51.011	176.433	11
97	Chad Little	John Deere Ford	51.354	175.254	16
05	Morgan Shepherd	Delco Remy Pontiac	51.656	174.230	18
31	Mike Skinner	Lowe's Chevy	50.373	178.667	4
62	Jeff Davis	Big Daddy's Bar-B-Que Ford	52.496	171.442	20
10	Ricky Rudd	Tide Ford	50.525	178.130	7
43	John Andretti	STP Pontiac	50.427	178.476	7
23	Jimmy Spencer	The Winston Ford	51.112	176.084	17
99	Jeff Burton	Exide Batteries Ford	50.551	178.038	9
14	Boris Said	Federated Auto Parts Ford	51.629	174.321	23
1	Steve Park	Pennzoil Chevy	51.158	175.926	20
	(Bumps #62 Davis)				
44	Kyle Petty	Hot Wheels Pontiac	50.691	177.546	14
	(Bumps #05 Shepherd)				
88	Dale Jarrett	Quality Care Service/Ford Credit Ford	50.319	178.859	3
	(Bumps #14 Said)				
30	Derrike Cope	Jimmy Dean Pontiac	50.895	176.835	17
	(Bumps #00 Jones)				

Car #	Driver	Team	Time	MPH	Pos
77	Robert Pressley (Bumps #97 Little)	Jasper Engines & Transmissions Ford	50.698	177.522	16
20	Tony Stewart (Bumps #16 Lepage)	The Home Depot Pontiac	50.463	178.348	9
21	Elliott Sadler (Bumps #1 Park)	CITGO Petroleum Corp. Ford	50.520	178.147	10
4	Bobby Hamilton	Kodak Film Chevy	52.210	172.381	DNQ
36	Ernie Irvan	M & M's Pontiac	51.393	175.121	DNQ
45	Rich Bickle (Bumps #32 M. Wallace)	10-10-345 Lucky Dog P.C. Pontiac	51.035	176.350	22
90	Stanton Barrett	Hills Bros./'Nestle' Ford	51.625	174.334	DNQ
55	Kenny Wallace	Square D Chevy	51.391	175.128	DNQ
11	Brett Bodine	Paychex Ford	51.352	175.261	DNQ
01	Jeff Green	TRACFONE Chevy	51.231	175.675	DNQ
18	Bobby Labonte (Bumps #23 Spencer)	Interstate Batteries Pontiac	50.380	178.642	6
93	Dave Blaney (Bumps #98 Mast)	Amoco Pontiac	50.645	177.708	16
75	Ted Musgrave (Bumps #91 Trickle)	Remington Arms Ford	51.056	176.277	25
9	Jerry Nadeau (Bumps #75 Musgrave)	Cartoon Network Ford	50.806	177.144	21
5	Terry Labonte (Bumps #45 Bickle)	Kellogg's Chevy	50.664	177.641	18
25	Wally Dallenbach Jr. (Bumps #58 Stricklin)	Budweiser Chevy	50.765	177.288	22
61	Bob Strait	Midway Island Ford	52.624	171.025	DNQ
42	Joe Nemechek	BellSouth Chevy	50.970	176.574	DNQ
41	David Green (Bumps #30 Cope)	Kodiak Chevy	50.307	178.902	3
22	Ward Burton (Bumps #71 Marcis)	Caterpillar Pontiac	50.470	178.324	12
80	Gary Bradberry	Stan Hover Motorsports Ford	51.930	173.310	DNQ
28	Kenny Irwin (Bumps #9 Nadeau)	Texaco/Havoline Ford	50.547	178.052	15
50	Ricky Craven (Bumps #25 Dallenbach)	Midwest Transit Chevy	50.716	177.459	25
3	Dale Earnhardt (Bumps #50 Craven)	GM Goodwrench Service Plus Chevy	50.570	177.971	18
26	Johnny Benson	Cheerios Ford	51.521	174.686	DNQ
66	Darrell Waltrip	Big Kmart/Route 66 Ford	50.998	176.478	DNQ

* New Track Record

25

SECOND-ROUND QUALIFYING

Musgrave's 176.943 mph is The Best of The Rest

By Al Pearce

For many teams, the decision to requalify for the Brickyard 400 was fairly simple. They were teams that felt with some degree of certainty they would run faster in Friday's second session than they had in Thursday's first; were out of provisionals and had little choice; or had been so slow on Thursday they couldn't reasonably expect to make the field by standing on their time.

Sixteen teams fell into one or more of those categories. The other 14 that hadn't qualified on Thursday elected to stand on their times and hope for the best. (Seven of them were high enough in owner points to have provisionals as a safety net).

Some of the sport's better-known drivers were in line when Round 2 began at 12:05 P.M. Among them: 1994 Brickyard 400 pole-winner Rick Mast, 1994 race runner-up Brett Bodine, two-time pole-winner Ernie Irvan, second-year driver Steve Park, and veterans Morgan Shepherd, Dick Trickle, Ted Musgrave, and Mike Wallace.

With Pennzoil one of the Brickyard 400's official sponsors, Steve Park was feeling the pressure after failing to make the 25-car cut in first-round qualifying. Things went better on Friday, when Park made the field with room to spare.

There were two driver changes prior to the session: Steve Grissom replaced Busch Series title-hopeful Jeff Green in the No. 01 Chevrolet, and Lance Hooper replaced Jeff Davis in the No. 62 Ford. Green had Busch Series obligations at nearby Indianapolis Raceway Park, and after being slow all week, Davis felt Hooper might find enough speed on Friday to make the field.

As usual, the weather played a role. It was 68 degrees Fahrenheit with 73-percent humidity when the morning session began at 9:04 A.M. Those ideal conditions helped 10 drivers record their fastest laps of the week. Among them were second-round hopefuls Musgrave, Shepherd, Mast, Park, Bodine, road racer Boris Said, and Stanton Barrett.

But the temperature rose to 80 degrees Fahrenheit and the humidity was 41 percent when Round 2 began. Musgrave, the second driver out, easily moved into the field with a lap of 176.946 miles per hour. After Grissom, Bodine, Barrett, and Irvan failed to qualify, Park secured a place on the grid at 176.744 miles per hour. None of the next seven drivers made it: Said, Hooper, Gary Bradberry, Shepherd, Kevin Lepage, Wallace, or Trickle. Mast, the last driver in line, easily made the field with a lap of 176.512 miles per hour.

Musgrave's run moved him from 35th overall to 30th on the grid. Park (who had been fastest in the morning session) advanced from 40th to 32nd, and

Don't blame Ernie Irvan for looking tense. The former Brickyard 400 polesitter had never been at a loss for speed at Indianapolis until this August, when he had to rely on a provisional starting position to make the field.

Mast improved from 37th to 34th. That was sweet news, indeed, for their teams. But while these three teams celebrated making the field, Rich Bickle, owner T. J. Beverley, and their crew were stunned to realize they were going home early.

After placing 34th in Thursday's first session (at 176.350 miles per hour), Bickle's team decided to stand on that speed. Even though Bickle's best lap in Friday practice had been 177.294 miles per hour—easily fast enough to make the field—both Bickle and his crew felt that since that lap had come in the cool of the morning that he would not be able to duplicate it when the second qualifying session began shortly after noon.

Nobody ran nearly that fast, but they didn't have to. Musgrave pushed Bickle down to 35th on the grid, Park pushed him to 36th, then Mast's session-ending lap pushed him to 37th and out of the race. "We thought the track would be slower [for Round 2], so we stood on our time," Bickle said. "We tested well here and brought back the same car, but there was something wrong with the trailing arm. We missed the race by 0.024 of a second. That's tough to take."

Eight of the other 13 who stood on their time stayed among the top 36: Ricky Craven, Wally Dallenbach Jr., Jerry Nadeau, Dave Marcis, Derrike Cope, and Joe Nemechek, as well as three-time series champion Darrell Waltrip who was kicked from 32nd to 35th, and Hut Stricklin who dropped from 33rd to 36th. At 176.433 miles per hour, Stricklin was the last driver to make the race on speed. And just how close was it?

Stricklin was a mere .083 miles per hour faster and .024 seconds quicker than Bickle for 36th on the grid.

NASCAR awarded owner-point provisionals to fill positions 37 through 43. The positions went to Bobby Hamilton, Chad Little, Johnny Benson, Irvan, Kenny Wallace, Jimmy Spencer, and Lepage.

Eleven drivers missed the field: Bickle, Bodine (his first DNQ since 1997), Said, Trickle, Grissom, Shepherd, Hooper, Barrett, Mike Wallace, Bradberry, and Bob Strait. After placing 48th in Round 1 qualifying and only 23rd in the Friday morning practice session, rookie Buckshot Jones withdrew his entry and didn't attempt to run the second qualifying session.

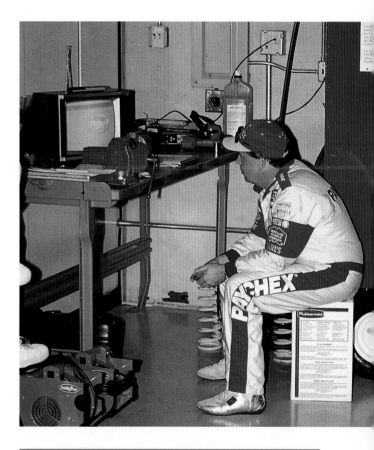

Above left **Kevin Lepage (left) and his crew struggled throughout the practice and qualifying sessions to coax speed out of their Roush Ford. Lepage ended up taking the final provisional starting spot and lined up 43rd.**

Above **A study in dejection: as qualifying winds down, Brett Bodine gazes at a closed-circuit TV monitor, coming to grips with the sad fact that his car was not fast enough to secure a position in the Brickyard 400.**

Second-Round Qualifying Results
6th Brickyard 400
Indianapolis Motor Speedway • NASCAR Winston Cup Series

Standing on Times

Car	Driver	Car Name	Time	Speed	Speed Rank
50	Ricky Craven	Midwest Transit Chevrolet	50.716	177.459	
25	Wally Dallenbach, Jr.	Budweiser Chevrolet	50.765	177.288	
9	Jerry Nadeau	Cartoon Network Ford	50.806	177.144	
71	Dave Marcis	Realtree Chevrolet	50.825	177.078	
30	Derrike Cope	Jimmy Dean Pontiac	50.895	176.835	
42	Joe Nemechek	BellSouth Chevrolet	50.970	176.574	
66	Darrell Waltrip	Big Kmart/Route 66 Ford	50.998	176.478	
58	Hut Stricklin	MTX Audio/CT Farms Ford	51.011	176.433	
45	Rich Bickle	10-10-345 Lucky Dog Pontiac	51.035	176.350	
23	Jimmy Spencer	The Winston Ford	51.112	176.084	
97	Chad Little	John Deere Ford	51.354	175.254	
55	Kenny Wallace	Square D Chevrolet	51.391	175.128	
26	Johnny Benson	Cheerios Ford	51.521	174.686	
4	Bobby Hamilton	Kodak Film Chevrolet	52.210	172.381	

T.O.D.	Qual.	Car	Driver	Car Name	Time	Speed	Rank
12:00 AM	0	61	Bob Strait	Midway Island Ford	0.000	0.000	0
			(Spun in Turn 4, no time)				
12:05 PM	2	75	Ted Musgrave	Remington Arms Ford	50.863	176.946	30
			(Bumps #97 Little)				
12:08 PM	3	01	Steve Grissom	TRACFONE Chevrolet	51.738	173.953	DNQ
12:00 AM	0	11	Brett Bodine	Paychex Ford	0.000	0.000	0
12:12 PM	5	90	Stanton Barrett	Hills Bros./Nestle' Ford	51.948	173.250	DNQ
12:16 PM	6	36	Ernie Irvan	M & M's Pontiac	51.271	175.538	DNQ
12:14 PM	7	1	Steve Park	Pennzoil Chevrolet	50.921	176.744	32
			(Bumps #23 Spencer)				
12:00 AM	0	14	Boris Said	Federated Auto Parts Ford	0.000	0.000	0
12:20 PM	9	62	Lance Hooper	Big Daddy's Bar-B-Que Ford	51.905	173.394	DNQ
12:22 PM	10	80	Gary Bradberry	Stan Hover Motorsports Ford	52.564	171.220	DNQ
12:25 PM	11	05	Morgan Shepherd	Delco Remy Pontiac	51.859	173.548	DNQ
12:26 PM	12	16	Kevin Lepage	TV Guide Ford	51.392	175.125	DNQ
12:28 PM	13	32	Mike Wallace	Ultra Wheels Ford	52.159	172.549	DNQ
12:30 PM	14	91	Dick Trickle	All INVINCA-Shield Chevrolet	51.667	174.192	DNQ
12:31 PM	15	98	Rick Mast	Team Woody Ford	50.988	176.512	34
			(Bumps #45 Bickle)				
	16	00	Buckshot Jones	Crown Fiber Pontiac	0.000	0.000	0
			(Withdrew, did not attempt)				

Starting Line-Up
6th Brickyard 400

Indianapolis Motor Speedway • NASCAR Winston Cup Series

	SP	CAR	YR	DRIVER	CAR NAME	Time	Speed
Row 1	1	24	5W	Jeff Gordon	DuPont Automotive Finishes Chevrolet	50.108	179.612*
	2	6	5	Mark Martin	Valvoline Ford	50.296	178.941
Row 2	3	41	1	David Green	Kodiak Chevrolet	50.307	178.902
	4	88	5W	Dale Jarrett	Quality Care Service/Ford Credit Ford	50.319	178.859
Row 3	5	7	5	Michael Waltrip	Philips Electronics Chevrolet	50.331	178.816
	6	31	2	Mike Skinner	Lowe's Chevrolet	50.373	178.667
Row 4	7	18	5	Bobby Labonte	Interstate Batteries Pontiac	50.380	178.642
	8	94	5	Bill Elliott	McDonald's Ford	50.407	178.547
Row 5	9	33	5	Ken Schrader	Skoal Chevrolet	50.415	178.518
	10	43	5	John Andretti	STP Pontiac	50.427	178.476
Row 6	11	20	#R	Tony Stewart	The Home Depot Pontiac	50.463	178.348
	12	22	5	Ward Burton	Caterpillar Pontiac	50.470	178.324
Row 7	13	21	#R	Elliott Sadler	CITGO Petroleum Corp. Ford	50.520	178.147
	14	10	5W	Ricky Rudd	Tide Ford	50.525	178.130
Row 8	15	28	1	Kenny Irwin	Texaco/Havoline Ford	50.547	178.052
	16	99	5	Jeff Burton	Exide Batteries Ford	50.551	178.038
Row 9	17	2	5	Rusty Wallace	Miller Lite Ford	50.566	177.985
	18	3	5W	Dale Earnhardt	GM Goodwrench Service Plus Chevrolet	50.570	177.971
Row 10	19	12	5	Jeremy Mayfield	Mobil 1 Ford	50.583	177.925
	20	93	#	Dave Blaney	Amoco Pontiac	50.645	177.708
Row 11	21	40	5	Sterling Marlin	Coors Light Chevrolet	50.661	177.651
	22	5	5	Terry Labonte	Kellogg's Chevrolet	50.664	177.641
Row 12	23	60	4	Geoffrey Bodine	PowerTeam Chevrolet	50.668	177.627
	24	44	5	Kyle Petty	Hot Wheels Pontiac	50.691	177.546
Row 13	25	77	3	Robert Pressley	Jasper Engines & Transmissions Ford	50.698	177.522
	26	50	4	Ricky Craven	Midwest Transit Chevrolet	50.716	177.459
Row 14	27	25	4	Wally Dallenbach, Jr.	Budweiser Chevrolet	50.765	177.288
	28	9	1	Jerry Nadeau	Cartoon Network Ford	50.806	177.144
Row 15	29	71	3	Dave Marcis	Realtree Chevrolet	50.825	177.078
	30	75	5	Ted Musgrave	Remington Arms Ford	50.863	176.946
Row 16	31	30	4	Derrike Cope	Jimmy Dean Pontiac	50.895	176.835
	32	1	1	Steve Park	Pennzoil Chevrolet	50.921	176.744
Row 17	33	42	5	Joe Nemechek	BellSouth Chevrolet	50.970	176.574
	34	98	5	Rick Mast	Team Woody Ford	50.988	176.512
Row 18	35	66	5	Darrell Waltrip	Big Kmart/Route 66 Ford	50.998	176.478
	36	58	3	Hut Stricklin	MTX Audio/CT Farms Ford	51.011	176.433
Row 19	37	4	5	Bobby Hamilton	Kodak Film Chevrolet	Provisional	
	38	97	2	Chad Little	John Deere Ford	Provisional	
Row 20	39	26	3	Johnny Benson	Cheerios Ford	Provisional	
	40	36	4	Ernie Irvan	M & M's Pontiac	Provisional	
Row 21	41	55	4	Kenny Wallace	Square D Chevrolet	Provisional	
	42	23	5	Jimmy Spencer	The Winston Ford	Provisional	
Row 22	43	16	#	Kevin Lepage	TV Guide Ford	Provisional	

* New track record: old mark, 179.394 mph by Ernie Irvan, August 1, 1998

1999 36-Car Field Average: 177.780   1998 36-Car Average: 176.445   **Difference: +1.335**

Field by Make of Car: Chevrolet - 16; Ford - 19; Pontiac - 8

Legend: W-Former Winner (4); #-First Time Brickyard 400 Starter (4); R-NASCAR Rookie (2)

Open-Wheel WIZARDS

Gordon and Stewart Lead the Charge into NASCAR's Upper Echelon

By Dave Argabright

O n a hot August morning in Indianapolis, a colorful bevy of Winston Cup cars roll onto the grid at the Indianapolis Motor Speedway, ready for one of stock car racing's most prestigious contests, the Brickyard 400.

A handful of the 43 drivers who made the show for 1999 share roots with the famous speedway. Like the Indianapolis Motor Speedway itself, these drivers origins stem from open wheel racing. In fact, these open wheel wizards are more than just competitors; they comprise some of the hottest young talent in NASCAR.

Opposite **Here's enough driving talent for any race, open-wheeled or fendered: Tony Stewart leads John Andretti around Turn 2 during the Brickyard 400.**

Jeff Gordon, Tony Stewart, Kenny Irwin Jr., John Andretti, Ken Schrader, and Dave Blaney all began their careers racing open-wheel cars in the Midwest. Today, they are the leaders of a cultural shift in stock car racing that has teams looking north for new talent. These six drivers have led the way and their transition has already changed the face of motorsports, especially stock car racing.

Once looked upon by many as a sport of the old South, it is no mystery that Gordon's arrival in NASCAR in the early 1990s helped spur the series' tremendous growth in mass appeal. Stewart threatens to be even bigger, as he is enjoying a phenomenal Winston Cup rookie season in 1999.

Although all six drivers have charismatic personalities, the key has been their ability to go fast in stock cars—shocking many, because in theory, their open-wheel roots haven't provided the experience needed to handle the big, heavy stock cars. But, it appears that theory is evolving. It is now believed that sprint cars and midgets offer an inviting background for a driver because those cars tend to be high-horsepower, lightweight, and very difficult to drive. So while a driver is spending years honing the reflexes and courage needed to go fast in open-wheel cars, he is also building skills that he can easily transfer to stock cars.

A pair of popular racers with Indianapolis ties, John Andretti and Tony Stewart share a moment between Brickyard practice sessions. Both men logged plenty of laps on the area's short tracks.

Jeff Gordon, who spent his formative years thrashing around the short tracks of Indiana aboard sprint cars and midgets, remains a popular figure in the area. Check out the collection of national and local media waiting to interview Jeff after his qualifying run!

"Probably the biggest thing about sprint cars and midgets is that you're always out of control," said Irwin, who drives the Texaco Havoline No. 28 for Robert Yates Racing. "You learn to race a little bit out of control, and after a while you get comfortable with it.

"You're truly running right on the edge of disaster all the time, and you kind of get your brain disciplined to that. It's very fun and exciting, but it definitely isn't easy. So when you get into a big stock car, it seems slow. That means that one of the things that can come

Jeff Gordon (4) and Rich Vogler (1) go wheel-to-wheel in USAC Sprint Cars on the high banks of the Winchester Speedway in Indiana on May 19, 1990. This fierce rivalry came to an end when Vogler lost his life at the Salem Speedway, only two months after this photo was taken. *John Mahoney*

A young Jeff Gordon aboard a USAC Sprint Car at Winchester Speedway on June 16, 1990. *John Mahoney*

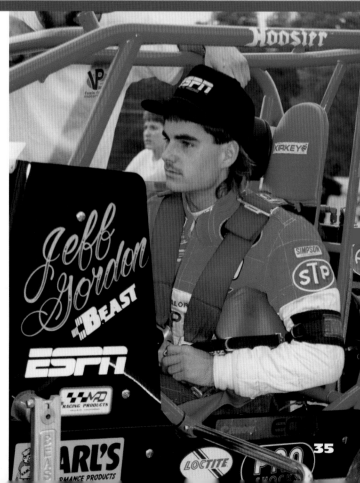

Jeff Gordon also spent some time behind the wheel of a USAC Silver Crown car, and is shown here at the wheel at Eldora Speedway. *John Mahoney*

naturally to you is the feel, because you're not scared out of your wits. We've learned to ignore the scared part and focus on the feel of the car."

One interesting angle for Andretti, Gordon, and Stewart is that they all credit Rollie Helmling, a Vincennes, Indiana, businessman, with playing a big role in their early success. Andretti remembers him from the beginning of his career:

"I ran one year in midgets and then I began driving for Rollie the next year," he recalled. "We had a lot of success together, and we became really good friends and we continue to be really good friends. I admire Rollie a lot, he's somebody who has helped a lot of young drivers come up through the ranks. He's got a really good eye [for young talent]."

After Andretti's departure from Helmling's team, Gordon took the seat. It was a picture-perfect match as Gordon's stock soared in Helmling's midget.

"Rollie saved my career, that's for sure," said Gordon. "I had just gotten fired from a sprint car ride. Bob East [who builds the Beast chassis], he was really getting popular with his cars and my stepfather, John Bickford, was building race-car parts at the time. They kind of came together and we got introduced to Rollie, and he was putting a new Beast midget together for the Night Before the 500 [at Indianapolis Raceway Park], and was looking for a driver. I happened to be at the right place at the right time.

"We went out there, set a new track record, and won the race. So that changed my career drastically,

immediately. I think that race was on television and it really got me interested in the [ESPN Thunder] series at IRP and Winchester and Salem. Next thing I know, we had a sprint car ourselves and continued to drive for Rollie and won a USAC midget championship in Belleville. And he is a great guy. A super guy, one of the nicest guys you'll ever meet."

After Gordon moved south, Stewart took the seat. One year later, Helmling decided to retire as a car owner. Stewart smiles when he thinks about the timing. "I guess I was the last guy. John got him started, Jeff wore him out, and I just destroyed him at the end of the deal," he laughed.

"He spent so much money on Jeff that he didn't have much money left when I drove the car," he continued, poking fun at Gordon.

"I won my first Hut Hundred driving for Rollie at Terre Haute. You know, there's not many guys like Rollie Helmling coming around. When you get a car owner like that and have the track record that he's had, you just . . . you're proud to be a part of his organization. That one year I drove for Rollie led to the year that I ran with Ralph Potter and won the national championship, and next year won the championship for Steve Lewis. So probably one of the biggest turning points for my career was running for Rollie."

Blaney, whose appearance at the Brickyard 400 was the third of five scheduled Winston Cup appearances in 1999, has spent the past two seasons on the Busch Grand National series. His roots are of a slightly

Tony Stewart's entrance into Winston Cup racing was one of the most successful debuts in modern times. By the time the Speedway opened for its Brickyard festivities, Stewart had already established himself as a top-notch stock car pilot and was cruising toward Winston Cup Rookie of the Year honors.

Tony Stewart left the seat of Team Menard's IRL car to move to Winston Cup competition. Shown here at the Indy 500 in 1997 with chief mechanic Larry Curry, Stewart won the season championship that year. *John Mahoney*

different flavor than the other open-wheel veterans because Blaney earned his stripes in a winged World of Outlaws sprint car.

The Cortland, Ohio, driver admits that racing at Indianapolis was a very distant dream as a young man.

"I never really thought much about Indy as a kid," he said. "I grew up racing on dirt, and when I was just 21 or so, I lucked into an opportunity to run a Silver Crown car in 1984 [he won the USAC Silver Crown championship that season]. But I really didn't think about moving on to run the Indianapolis 500. In 1984, nobody was moving from sprint cars and Silver Crown cars to Indianapolis, anyway. So I didn't spend any time thinking about it."

As Blaney plans his transition to Winston Cup from the Busch cars, he says people often caution him about the "tough transition" to Cup cars. He means no disrespect, he says, but he has to chuckle at their idea of "transition."

"Sprint cars to stock cars, man, you can't get any more different than that," he laughs. "I've been real polite and quiet sometimes when I sort of point that out to people, but I'm telling you, the transition from Busch to Cup is nothing compared to the transition I've already made from sprints to stock cars.

"I enjoy the Cup cars more because they have more horsepower, and that seems much more familiar to me. That's all I've ever driven, overpowered race cars. And you can call Winston Cup cars overpowered because they have more power than the tires can handle."

Schrader, who was one of the first open-wheel drivers to head south, says that his days in a sprint car and midget helped him learn to race. But he says that the best training ground may well be the USAC Silver Bullet series.

Unlike sprint car and midget races, Silver Bullet events are longer, sometimes 100 miles in length. Pit

At the USAC Sprints held at Salem, Indiana, Tony Stewart flies over the wall after crashing with Steve Butler (69). Stewart was uninjured, and found another car to drive in the feature. *John Mahoney*

stops usually take a driver out of contention, so the same set of tires often must last for the entire race. Also, the cars carry large 75-gallon fuel tanks—enough fuel is on board to go the entire distance. As the fuel load burns off, the handling of the car changes.

"Some of their races are on asphalt, and that's another big factor," says Schrader of the series. "But the big thing with those cars is that there is way too much weight, and too much horsepower for the tires.

"That series taught me a lot. You have to run the car as fast as you can, as straight as you can. And you have to constantly take care of your tires. You have to abuse them some, but not completely, because then they go away too quickly. It's a really tough thing to learn. And that's the whole stock car thing: Learning how to take care of every set of tires, and saving them to race at the right time."

Schrader looks back with fondness at his days in the Midwest.

"Those were good days," he says. "The first time I won a USAC midget race I won $600, and I thought

that was good, too. But today's times are also pretty good, too, even though we haven't won in a while.

"But I learned a lot back then. And I tried to not have to learn things more than once. I can think about times where I might have screwed up, or used up my tires too soon, and I would think afterwards, 'Well, that's the last time I'll do that.'

"When I started out I was just carrying a helmet, begging for rides, so I was super careful in the cars. Later on, when I got more aggressive, that's when it was more fun, and I learned more. Like I said, those were good days."

These days, stock car drivers work in a world of multi-million-dollar teams, driving flashy, famous race cars. And drivers such as Schrader, Gordon, Stewart, Andretti, Irwin, and Blaney have a long, secure future in the sport.

They can share their memories of growing up in the rough and rowdy world of open-wheel racing. It was a good education, they'll tell you. It made them what they are: stars that will shine for a long, long time.

Tony Stewart aboard a USAC midget at Terre Haute on June 9, 1995. *John Mahoney*

Opposite Tony Stewart and car owner Rollie Helmling at Indianapolis Raceway Park on June 12, 1993. Helmling played key roles in developing the careers of many upcoming drivers. Stewart, Jeff Gordon, and John Andretti all drove Helmling's USAC cars. *John Mahoney*

John Andretti at the wheel of a
midget at Terre Haute on July 27,
1985. *John Mahoney*

John Andretti drives a sprint car at Terre Haute on August 25, 1985. *John Mahoney*

Local boy John Andretti, a veteran of both Indy 500 and Brickyard 400 action at his hometown track, joined sportscaster Ed Sorenson for some on-camera duty over the 1999 Brickyard weekend.

Kenny Irwin obliges a portion of his Indiana constituency. An Indianapolis native, Irwin was the 1996 USAC national midget champion and a frequent winner throughout the Midwest.

Below Kenny Irwin wins a USAC Silver Crown race at Indianapolis Raceway Park on July 30, 1997.
John Mahoney

wynn's

4

Below left At the Hut Hundred in Terre Haute, Ken Schrader pilots a midget on September 9, 1979.
John Mahoney

Below right One of the first open-wheel pilots to make significant inroads into NASCAR Winston Cup racing, Ken Schrader still competes regularly on the short tracks of Mid-America and remains a favorite of Brickyard fans.

Ken Schrader just before setting the fast lap of the night at Winchester Speedway in Indiana. The car is a Hamilton Roadster Midget, the night was October 20, 1979. *John Mahoney*

Top Dave Blaney in St. Paul, Minnesota, on August 24, 1984—the year he won the Silver Crown title (his first season in the series). *John Mahoney*

Above Dave Blaney, the sprint car champion and budding NASCAR star, receives well-wishes from Indianapolis Motor Speedway president Tony George and Speedway chairman Mari Hulman George.

Right Dave Blaney at the wheel of a World of Outlaw sprint car at Bloomington, Indiana, on April 20, 1995. *John Mahoney*

Early on, the trio of Mark Martin, Jeff Gordon, and Dale Jarrett established themselves as the drivers to watch. Between them, this trio led all but three of the Brickyard's 160 laps.

THE BRICKYARD 400

BRICKYARD 400 — INDIANAPOLIS MOTOR SPEEDWAY

INDIANAPOLIS MOTOR SPEEDWAY

D.J. Delivers

Jarrett Displays Championship Form and Dominates the Sixth Brickyard 400

By Al Pearce

Before you can truly understand and appreciate the emotions surrounding Dale Jarrett's victory in the 1999 Brickyard 400, you must understand and appreciate the emotions the team experienced after it lost the 1998 race at the Indianapolis Motor Speedway.

In that event—and about this, there is little serious debate—Jarrett commanded the day's fastest and best-handling car. After qualifying second to Ernie Irvan, the 1996 Brickyard 400 Pole winner, he ran no lower than 3rd throughout the first third of the 160-lap,

This is the final pitstop, 14 laps from the finish. When Jarrett mashed the gas on the final restart and took off, the Brickyard 400 became a race for 2nd place. In the remaining distance, Jarrett built a lead of more than three seconds.

400-mile race. He took the lead at Lap 54, and easily held it until a series of misjudgments and gaffes conspired to cost him four laps and any chance of victory.

First, at Lap 77, the Pontiac of Ward Burton ran out of gas and stalled on the warm-up lane along the backstretch. Jarrett, himself due for a scheduled fuel and tire stop within a few laps, hesitated to pit until the caution flag waved. So he kept soldiering on, even though he was precariously close to running out of fuel.

NASCAR officials were loath to display the yellow flag, and held out hope Burton could bump-start his car to the pits without needing help. But those few moments of indecision cost Jarrett dearly. Coming for the cross flags signaling halfway, his Robert Yates-owned Ford Quality Care-sponsored No. 88 Ford Taurus sputtered and also ran out of gas.

Unlike Burton's, Jarrett's car managed to coast around to the entrance to pit road. By the time he got

there, Jarrett was already two laps down. And by the time his crewmen (with help from teammate Kenny Irwin's crewmen) pushed him to his pit, he had lost another two laps. Jarrett doggedly made up the four-lap deficit but had to settle for 16th when he simply ran out of laps.

Jarrett, Yates, and crew chief Todd Parrott lived with that costly and embarrassing mistake for the better part of a year. "How could you do it?" they heard time and again. You had the best car, so why get greedy and wait for a caution to pit? How will you get over it?

Whether they got over it—indeed, whether they'll *ever* get over it—is now a moot point. Robert Yates Racing exorcised the haunting memory of losing that Brickyard 400 by dominating the 1999 edition. Jarrett qualified 4th behind Jeff Gordon, Mark Martin, and David Green, then led six times for 117 of the 160 laps. His margin of victory over runner-up Bobby Labonte was 3.351 seconds, the largest in the six runnings of the annual midsummer Winston Cup race.

"And we did it with the same car we brought here last year," Jarrett said after his $712,240 payday. "What an incredible race car—and thank goodness, we were able to maybe make people forget about last year. The car was easy to drive because it handled perfectly and the engine was something else. We seem to have an awfully good package for this race track."

With the largest crowd of the Winston Cup season looking on, front-row starters Jeff Gordon and Mark Martin lead the field toward Turn 1 at the start of the sixth annual Brickyard 400.

Jarrett never ran lower than 3rd except during scheduled exchanges of pit stops. He moved from 4th to 3rd on the first lap, to 2nd on Lap 14, then took the lead when he and 3rd-running Martin went by Gordon at Lap 27. When Martin took the point to earn five lap-leader bonus points, Jarrett didn't put up much of a struggle. With his first service stop scheduled within 10 laps, Jarrett felt his crew would help him regain the lead with a quick stop.

And so it was. The round of green-flag stops between Laps 34 and 39 briefly shuffled the lineup, but No. 88 was again atop the scoring pylon when all the stops were done. His number stayed there for Laps 40–63, when Martin showed some muscle by passing in Turn 1. Two laps later, Jarrett easily regained the lead and effortlessly pulled away.

Other than Dave Marcis (Lap 75 during an exchange of pit stops), Bobby Labonte (on the restart at Lap 78), and Jeff Burton (during an exchange of pit stops at Lap 117), Jarrett led the final 85 laps. A caution at Lap 143 for Marcis' blown engine bunched the field, but the pursuers had no better luck handling Jarrett over the final 14 laps than they had had the previous 146 laps.

Most of the front-runners took two tires and a splash of gas under the last caution. The notable exceptions were Gordon (four tires) and Ward Burton (gas-and-go). The restart order at Lap 147 was Jarrett, Bobby Labonte, Ward Burton, Martin, Jeff Burton, Dale Earnhardt, Gordon, Terry Labonte, Tony Stewart, and Ricky Rudd. It took Jarrett only two laps to build almost a second lead over Ward Burton, who had passed Bobby Labonte on the restart.

As Jarrett steadily opened his lead, everyone from 2nd to 12th began fighting for leftovers. Bobby Labonte eventually got back by Ward Burton, although it was obvious he didn't have anything for Jarrett. Running on four fresh tires, Gordon charged from 8th to 3rd in the final 11 laps. In contrast, Ward Burton dropped from 2nd to 6th, Earnhardt went from 6th to 10th, and Terry Labonte slipped from 6th to 11th. The most productive late-race charge was Rusty Wallace's, from 13th on the restart to 8th at the finish.

When all was said and done—and just before light showers swept across the speedway—Jarrett ran easily ahead of Bobby Labonte, two-time Brickyard 400 winner Gordon, Martin, and Jeff Burton. The rest of the top 10 in the $6.1 million race were Ward Burton, rookie of the race Stewart, Wallace, 1997 race winner Rudd, and 1995 race winner Earnhardt. All told, 21 of the 43 starters finished on the lead lap, with another 11 finishers just one lap down.

There were no "ifs, ands, or buts" about this one. Wisely, none of the losers dared make excuses or claim they would have won except for this or that. Not only was Jarrett's win a record, but his 117 laps in front

Mark Martin appeared to badly want the early lead. Ignoring the widely held belief that the low line is the only route through Turn 1, Martin nosed ahead briefly by using the high groove. Alas, he could not make the move stick, and Jeff Gordon led the opening lap.

Early on, the trio of Mark Martin, Jeff Gordon, and Dale Jarrett established themselves as the drivers to watch. Between them, this trio led all but three of the Brickyard's 160 laps.

The notion that Indy is a one-groove track is challenged by Dale Earnhardt and Michael Waltrip, here trying to take the high road past Terry Labonte, Steve Park, and Elliott Sadler.

The downtown skyline looms in the distance; the towering grandstands along the South Chute at the Speedway loom over a string of NASCAR racers early in the Brickyard 400.

was 20 more than Gordon's previous laps-led record set in 1998.

From where Bobby Labonte sat, Jarrett's run was almost perfect. "He didn't slip or slide all day," he said. "He's got a really good line around this place, the smoothest I've ever seen. And he ran it all day. My car started missing right there at the end, but I don't think we would have caught him, anyway. He had a little better stuff; a better car and a better motor."

Gordon, who's dominated his share of races in recent years, knew a good butt-kicking when he saw one. "Except for qualifying, D.J. (Dale Jarrett) had us covered all weekend," he said. "Even in practice, I knew he was the guy to beat. I thought we had something for him, but our car went away on old tires. We were by far the best Chevrolet, but we didn't have anything for the 88. Really, we were about fifth-best, so we're happy to get a 3rd. A pole and a 3rd make for a pretty good weekend at Indy."

Martin came into the 400 hoping to cut into Jarrett's triple-digit point lead. He left as stoic and un-

emotional as ever. "We had the car to beat early-on, but the handle got away from us later on," he said. "At the end, we were faster than the 18 (Bobby Labonte), but couldn't get up to him. And we weren't as fast as the 88 or the 24 (Gordon), so we'll take 4th. It was a good run for us."

Jeff Burton's problems were more off the track than on. Uncharacteristically for a Roush Racing Team, his crew cost him six seconds during his first yellow-flag service stop, then struggled another time. It didn't help when he changed his mind in mid-stop (two tires instead of four) and almost drove off with the left-side lug nuts loose. "Before all that," he said, "I was gonna finish 2nd. But we lost too much track position. It's not like us to have a bad day in the pits, but we did and that really hurt us."

Ward Burton's no-tire stop moved him from 7th to 3rd in the pits, and he raced to 2nd before slipping back to 6th. Stewart's 7th was the best ever by a Brickyard 400 rookie; Wallace's 8th was his fifth top-10 in six IMS races; Rudd's 9th was his first top-10 of the season; and Earnhardt's 10th kept him solidly in the top-10 in points.

The race was slowed only three times for incidents. The first yellow came at Lap 44 when Geoffrey Bodine got into Chad Little in Turn 1, then hit him hard enough in Turn 2 to send Little into the wall. He was angry and frustrated, but otherwise fine. "I thought I gave him enough room," Little said, "but I guess I didn't. I just know I got hit."

Kyle Petty brought out the second caution when his car cut a right front tire at Lap 74 and slammed hard into the Turn 1 wall. "It hurt my feelings, that's about it," he said. "By the time I came to the corner, it was down and that was it." And the last caution was for Marcis' blown engine at Lap 143 that set up the 14-lap sprint to the finish.

The victory was Jarrett's fourth of 1999, the 22nd of his Winston Cup career. More important, it stretched his lead in the championship standings to 274 points with 14 races remaining. Among his 22 victories are two each in the Daytona 500 and Brickyard 400. And while he's not about to say the Brickyard 400 is bigger than the Daytona 500, it was clear that

he and his team were finally glad to put the 1998 debacle behind them.

"That [1998] was a tough deal, the kind of thing you hate to see happen on a day when you have the best car and the best opportunity to win," he said. "But when it was over, we knew we had to get ready to go race at Watkins Glen the next weekend. So we had to say, 'Hey, it's over.' We made a mistake in trying to guess what NASCAR was going to do with the caution flag, and it bit us. There was nothing we could do about it except learn from it."

Opposite **Track position is vital at the Speedway, hence this early land rush as drivers who qualified out of the first few rows try valiantly to stay in contact with the leaders.**

Below **One of the great battles in the race's opening stages involved John Andretti's Pontiac and the Ford of Kenny Irwin, here shown rocketing down the long front straightaway.**

Best seat in the house: Mike Skinner, lurking a few car-lengths back, stalks Kenny Irwin and John Andretti as they try two distinct lines around Turn 1.

Below Dale Earnhardt runs just ahead of Mike Skinner, who, judging by his aggressive move below the white line in the turn, is trying pretty hard to pass his partner in the Richard Childress Racing stable.

Parrott recalled that the flight back to North Carolina after the 1998 race wasn't a very cheery one. "Jarrett," he said, "sat up front, between the pilots, and said hardly a word." Parrott and some of the other crewmen were in the back, doing too much soul-searching to talk. "We felt bad about it and so did Dale," he said. "I was pretty low because it was a mistake that shouldn't have happened. Today is vindication. That's the best word for it, vindication."

Jarrett won a career-high seven races in 32 starts for Yates two years ago. It went for naught as he finished 2nd in points to Gordon, a 10-time winner. But Jarrett's on pace to win six or seven this year, a year in which almost everyone figures he'll be the Winston Cup champion for the first time in his career.

"This is one of those years when everything just clicks," he said at Indy. "I don't want anyone to shake me or wake me up because this is as good as it can get right now. I don't see us winning as many races as Jeff did the past two years (10 in 1997 and 13 last year), but if we keep running up front and getting top-fives, I think we've got a real chance at the championship."

Gordon agrees 100 percent. While unwilling to publicly say his Hendrick Motorsports Team can't win the Cup this year, the three-time and defending series champion sees "champions" written all over Jarrett and Robert Yates Racing. And if anyone should know what it takes, he does.

"They've been right there, 2nd or 3rd in the final standings many times," he said. "I think that team is very, very tough right now. Dale's on a pretty good roll and has been doing great. Our team isn't even thinking about Dale and his team. We're just trying to win some races and gain some points. We're in no position to even be thinking about making a run at another championship.

"It's like they were just biding their time, getting all those top-5s early in the season. Then, all of a sudden, everything started clicking for them. Boom! Now, they're getting wins and doing a great job. And they deserve it because they've worked hard. My team has got to get things going so we can make 'em work for it. Right now, it's too easy for 'em."

Jarrett crashed out of the season-opening Daytona 500, his only DNF in the season's first 20 races. He was 2nd the following weekend in Rockingham, then ran out of gas (again!) en route to an 11th place at Las Vegas the first Sunday in March. From then through the Brickyard 400, he scored 14 top-five and 16 top-ten finishes.

"They've got things clicking over there better than we did last year," said Gordon. "It certainly seems they've got it together sooner than we did at this point of last season. They know when to get a top-5, and

Steve Park flirts with the "rumble strips" inside Turn 1 in this fight with fellow Chevrolet driver Wally Dallenbach. Both ran the complete distance, with Dallenbach nosing out Park for the 14th finishing position.

when they're capable of winning, they go out there and do that, too. They're going to be tough to beat. In fact, I don't know if anybody can."

You're not going to get any argument from Jarrett. "It's a lot more fun and easier leading than chasing," he said. "When you're 2nd or 3rd in points, you have to rely on somebody else's problems for you to gain points. In the last couple of years there were many times we finished 2nd or 3rd or 4th, but the problem was that the guy ahead of us on the track that day was the guy ahead of us in points. Even when we finished 1st, he'd finish so we didn't gain that many points. That was frustrating."

And now? "It feels great knowing that as the point leader, we can finish 1st or 2nd, and gain points or not lose any," Jarrett said. "Teams chasing us in the standings see the races starting to count down, and they realize their time is running out. That's why it's a lot more fun to be in control of your own destiny."

Hot Wheels, indeed! Kyle Petty's ride had to be pretty hot just to keep pace with the surrounding traffic in the early stages of the Brickyard 400.

Right A 30-car conga line snakes its way down the long back straightaway at Indianapolis. Somewhere up there, more than half a mile or so away, is leader Jeff Gordon.

Below Green-flag stops shifted the crowd's focus from the front stretch to the pit lane, where the speeds were considerably slower but the action was no less intense.

Bottom Think leading the Brickyard 400 isn't important? Why else would Mark Martin be this low on the track, trying to pass Jeff Gordon? And why else would Gordon be trying so darned hard to keep Martin back there?

David Green, who hoped to be the Brickyard 400's Cinderella story after his marvelous qualifying run, prepares to surrender a position to the real prince of this year's event, Dale Jarrett.

Rookie Dave Blaney and veteran Bill Elliott streak across the "Yard of BrickS" that both marks the finish line at the Indianapolis Motor Speedway and gives the track's NASCAR event its name.

Above **Flexing his stock car muscles a bit, Winston Cup sophomore Kenny Irwin leads John Andretti, Dale Earnhardt, Jeff Burton, and—well, just about every driver in the starting field.**

Above right **The huge water tower welcoming visitors to the town of Speedway, the mammoth grandstands, the familiar VIP suites outside Turn 2; this can only be the Indianapolis Motor Speedway.**

Right **This Jerry Nadeau sandwich features Darrell Waltrip in the foreground and Ted Musgrave along the outer wall. All three men fared poorly in the 400, with Nadeau topping the trio in 31st at the finish.**

Above, left Crowds to the left, crowds to the right. Literally tens of thousands of spectators caught the first turn action up close and personal in the Brickyard 400.

Above, right Something old, something new: just inside Turn 2 of the famed old Speedway, one can see a portion of the Formula One road course that will be used in the United States Grand Prix, beginning in September 2000.

Below Between pit stops, the uniformed crewmen along pit road essentially did what a quarter-million other Brickyard attendees did: they watched as the Brickyard 400 unfolded.

In three full seasons with the Indy Racing League, Tony Stewart grew accustomed to being followed around the Indianapolis Motor Speedway. In the 1999 Brickyard 400, he learned how it felt in a stock car.

Below Mark Martin sets the pace, with Jeff Gordon in the chase role. Early on, Martin seemed to be the quicker of the pair, but Gordon had the speed when it counted and edged Martin for the 3rd finishing position.

Opposite Monkey see, monkey do. Each caution period saw the lead cars file on and off pit road virtually as a single unit. Here, Bobby Labonte leads the troops out the pit exit after service has been completed.

Right Slipping, sliding, looking for the lines that suit their cars best, a dozen drivers scramble through Turn 1. The lack of any real banking in the turns, combined with the high straightaway speeds, make Indianapolis a chassis man's nightmare.

How about a little sibling rivalry at, oh, 180 miles per hour? Ward Burton leads his brother Jeff into Turn 1 in the Brickyard 400. It was a good day for the favorite sons of South Boston, Virginia, with Jeff finishing 5th and Ward running a fine 6th.

Heading into the race, there was speculation that the Pontiac brigade—including Tony Stewart and John Andretti, shown here—would enjoy an aerodynamic edge at Indy. Alas, while both men ran well, neither managed to lead a lap in the Brickyard 400.

Dale Jarrett, Mark Martin, Jeff Burton, and company head down pit road for caution-period pit stops. Such visits were a rarity in this Brickyard 400; only three times did the yellow flag wave.

Quietly, and yet forcefully, Steve Park worked his way up from 32nd at the start of the Brickyard 400 to 15th when the checkered flag came down.

There are those who insist that the Indianapolis Motor Speedway is at the hub of the motorsports universe, and it certainly feels that way each August when the NASCAR folks come to town.

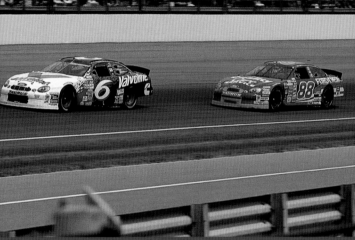

The fast Fords of Mark Martin and Dale Jarrett each had their moments as the fastest cars in the Brickyard field. Jarrett's timing was better; as he was faster when it counted most.

Chad Little's Ford gets winched up onto a roll-back wrecker bed after hard contact with the second-turn wall on Lap 44. Little was not hurt in the incident.

This isn't the way Darrell Waltrip wanted to exit the Brickyard 400. Waltrip, who will retire after the 2000 NASCAR Winston Cup season, ran just 58 laps before his Ford gave up the fight.

Above, left Seventeen laps from the finish, Dave Marcis was unable to steer his car off the track after its engine blew, setting the stage for the final caution period of the race.

Above, right It was a terrific day for Joe Gibbs Racing. While neither Bobby Labonte nor Tony Stewart could pull off a victory, they finished 2nd and 7th, respectively, each solidifying his top-5 position in the Winston Cup points standings.

Left Jeff Burton's day was a roller coaster. He started 16th and repeatedly raced his way toward the front, only to have recurring troubles on pit road. In the end, Jeff's steady drive was good enough for 5th place.

Mark Martin's crew was rock-solid all day, keeping it's man in the top five. Martin's crew was among the teams electing to change just two tires during the final caution flag.

Left Quick service: four tires, a full tank of gas, a quick cleaning of the grille by crew chief Robin Pemberton, and Rusty Wallace is ready to rejoin the Brickyard 400 en route to his 8th-place finish.

Above, left Tony Stewart was fast after the final round of pit stops and picked up several positions, but ran out of time once he had climbed into the 7th spot.

Above, right Dale Earnhardt had an up-and-down day, running well at times and fading at others. Toward the end, unfortunately, he was in fading mode, and had to settle for 10th at the checkers.

Below One of the day's steadiest performances was turned in by the Tide team and driver Ricky Rudd. The 1997 winner of the Brickyard 400, Rudd soldiered on to finish 9th in this year's edition.

Above left **Wally Dallenbach acquitted himself well in his fourth try at the Brickyard 400, finishing 14th in his Hendrick Motorsports Chevy after qualifying a disappointing 27th on Thursday.**

Above center **Now that's pressure! Jeff Gordon exits Indy's second turn with Dale Earnhardt's black Chevrolet looming large in his rear-view mirror and looking for passing room on the low side.**

Above right **David Green's Brickyard 400, while not exactly living up to the expectations forged by his 3rd-place qualifying run, was nonetheless a good one. David finished 20th, but was still on the lead lap when the checkered flag waved.**

A trail of sparks shows beneath Kyle Petty's car after a deflated right-front tire sent him into the first turn wall. The crash left Kyle 41st in the 1999 chapter of a race that has never been kind to him.

Above, left Nothing to do now but sit and wait . . . and maybe pray a little bit. As the laps wind down, Dale Jarrett's crewmen have done their jobs, and can only watch as he does his.

Above, right This is the final restart, 14 laps from the finish. When Jarrett mashed the gas and took off, the Brickyard 400 became a race for 2nd place. In the remaining distance, Jarrett built a lead of more than three seconds.

Here's a breathtaking moment: Ward Burton's Pontiac jumps sideways as he leaves Turn 2 behind him. Ken Schrader, trailing Burton, got an eyeful of this action.

White flag. Just one more lap. Four more corners. Two and a half miles. And, of course, a left turn into the most hallowed Victory Circle in motorsports, where prizes await totaling more than $700,000.

Last year, Dale Jarrett's team felt the bitter sting of defeat after running out of gas halfway through the Brickyard 400. This year, the team's calculations were perfect, as were their car and their driver.

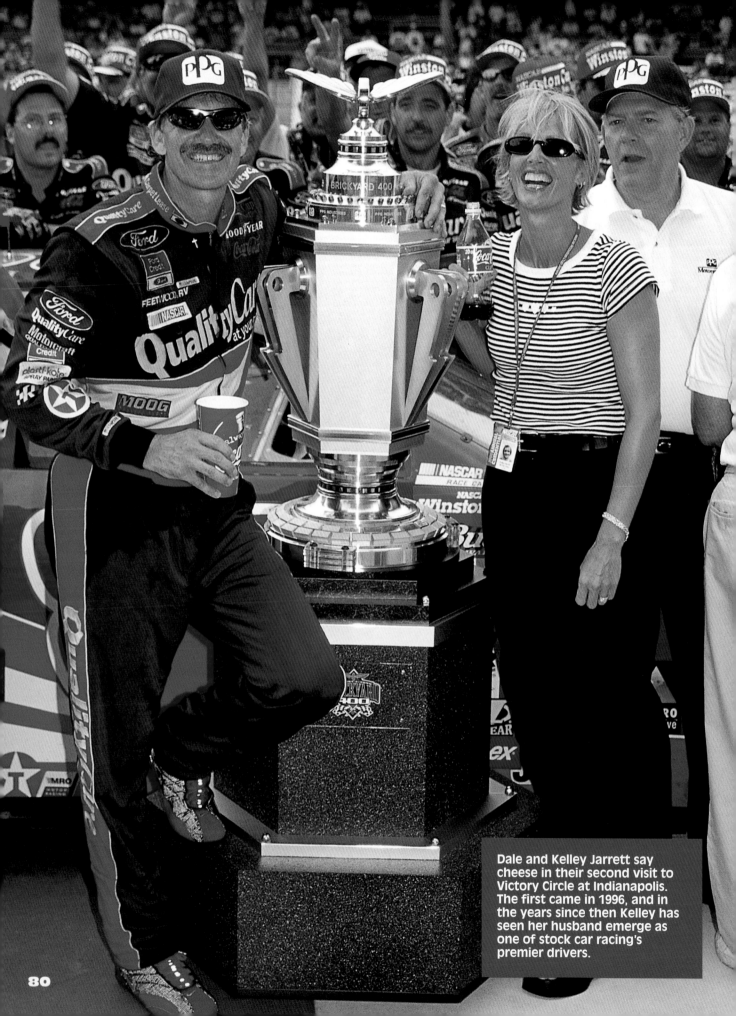

Dale and Kelley Jarrett say cheese in their second visit to Victory Circle at Indianapolis. The first came in 1996, and in the years since then Kelley has seen her husband emerge as one of stock car racing's premier drivers.

Box Score
6th Brickyard 400
Indianapolis Motor Speedway • NASCAR Winston Cup Series

FP	SP	Car	Yr	Driver	Car Name	Laps Comp	Running/ Reason Out	Prize Money
1	4	88	5W	Dale Jarrett	Quality Care Service/Ford Credit Ford	160	Running	$712,240
2	7	18	5	Bobby Labonte	Interstate Batteries Pontiac	160	Running	270,950
3	1	24	5W	Jeff Gordon	DuPont Automotive Finishes Chevrolet	160	Running	262,800
4	2	6	5	Mark Martin	Valvoline Ford	160	Running	222,450
5	16	99	5	Jeff Burton	Exide Batteries Ford	160	Running	193,240
6	12	22	5	Ward Burton	Caterpillar Pontiac	160	Running	157,210
7	11	20	#R	Tony Stewart	The Home Depot Pontiac	160	Running	162,635
8	17	2	5	Rusty Wallace	Miller Lite Ford	160	Running	140,435
9	14	10	5W	Ricky Rudd	Tide Ford	160	Running	137,535
10	18	3	5W	Dale Earnhardt	GM Goodwrench Service Plus Chevrolet	160	Running	135,525
11	22	5	5	Terry Labonte	Kellogg's Chevrolet	160	Running	129,160
12	6	31	2	Mike Skinner	Lowe's Chevrolet	160	Running	117,010
13	15	28	1	Kenny Irwin	Texaco/Havoline Ford	160	Running	111,410
14	27	25	4	Wally Dallenbach	Budweiser Chevrolet	160	Running	109,610
15	32	1	1	Steve Park	Pennzoil Chevrolet	160	Running	109,610
16	21	40	5	Sterling Marlin	Coors Light Chevrolet	160	Running	109,310
17	25	77	3	Robert Pressley	Jasper Engines & Transmissions Ford	160	Running	100,450
18	9	33	5	Ken Schrader	Skoal Chevrolet	160	Running	105,410
19	39	26	3	Johnny Benson	Cheerios Ford	160	Running	112,410
20	3	41	1	David Green	Kodiak Chevrolet	160	Running	101,575
21	13	21	#R	Elliott Sadler	CITGO Petroleum Corp. Ford	160	Running	102,710
22	33	42	5	Joe Nemechek	BellSouth Chevrolet	159	Running	100,710
23	8	94	5	Bill Elliott	McDonald's Ford	159	Running	99,610
24	40	36	4	Ernie Irvan	M & M's Pontiac	159	Running	98,510
25	23	60	4	Geoffrey Bodine	PowerTeam Chevrolet	159	Running	90,710
26	42	23	4	Jimmy Spencer	The Winston Ford	159	Running	96,385
27	5	7	5	Michael Waltrip	Philips Electronics Chevrolet	159	Running	94,885
28	20	93	#	Dave Blaney	Amoco Pontiac	159	Running	84,385
29	19	12	5	Jeremy Mayfield	Mobil 1 Ford	159	Running	98,885
30	43	16	#	Kevin Lepage	TV Guide Ford	159	Running	90,910
31	28	9	1	Jerry Nadeau	Cartoon Network Ford	159	Running	83,485
32	31	30	4	Derrike Cope	Jimmy Dean Pontiac	159	Running	82,385
33	36	58	3	Hut Stricklin	MTX Audio/CT Farms Ford	158	Running	82,135
34	26	50	4	Ricky Craven	Midwest Transit Chevrolet	158	Running	81,885
35	30	75	5	Ted Musgrave	Remington Arms Ford	158	Running	84,110
36	34	98	5	Rick Mast	Team Woody Ford	158	Running	81,510
37	10	43	5	John Andretti	STP Pontiac	158	Running	96,410
38	37	4	5	Bobby Hamilton	Kodak Film Chevrolet	157	Running	96,310
39	41	55	4	Kenny Wallace	Square D Chevrolet	157	Running	81,210
40	29	71	3	Dave Marcis	Realtree Chevrolet	139	Engine	82,010
41	24	44	5	Kyle Petty	Hot Wheels Pontiac	72	Accident	81,010
42	35	66	5	Darrell Waltrip	Big Kmart/Route 66 Ford	58	Handling	80,910
43	38	97	2	Chad Little	John Deere Ford	41	Accident	91,605

Time of Race: 2:41:57
Margin of Victory: 3.351 seconds
Legend: W: Former Brickyard 400 Winner   **R:** 1999 NASCAR Winston Cup Rookie   **#:** Brickyard 400 Rookie

Average Speed: 148.194 mph
Fastest Leading Lap: #88 Dale Jarrett, Lap 49, 171.795 mph

Lap Leaders

Laps	Leader
1–5	Jeff Gordon, #24
6–7	Mark Martin, #6
8–26	Jeff Gordon, #24
27	Dale Jarrett, #88
28–39	Mark Martin, #6
40–63	Dale Jarrett, #88
64–65	Mark Martin, #6
66–74	Dale Jarrett, #88
75	Dave Marcis, #71
76–77	Dale Jarrett, #88
78	Bobby Labonte, #18
79–116	Dale Jarrett, #88
117–117	Jeff Burton, #99
118–160	Dale Jarrett, #88

Lap Leader Recap

Lap Leader Recap	Number of Times Lead	Number of Laps Lead
Dale Jarrett	6	117
Jeff Gordon	2	24
Mark Martin	3	16
Bobby Labonte	1	1
Dave Marcis	1	1
Jeff Burton	1	1

Caution Flags 3 for 12 laps

44–47	(4) Accident Turn 2: #97
74–77	(4) Accident Turn 1: #44
143–146	(4) Engine: #71

NASCAR Winston Cup Points Report

1	Dale Jarrett	3,199
2	Mark Martin	2,925
3	Bobby Labonte	2,906
4	Jeff Burton	2,819
5	Tony Stewart	2,711
6	Jeff Gordon	2,692
7	Dale Earnhardt	2,601
8	Terry Labonte	2,378
9	Mike Skinner	2,368
10	Rusty Wallace	2,341

Race Position by 10-Lap Intervals

Car	Driver	SP	1	10	20	30	40	50	60	70	80	90	100	110	120	130	140	150	160	Driver
1	Steve Park	32	34	26	23	21	19	19	19	17	22	18	16	13	15	14	13	14	15	Steve Park
2	Rusty Wallace	17	18	19	17	17	13	12	13	10	10	9	9	9	8	9	9	9	8	Rusty Wallace
3	Dale Earnhardt	18	15	17	16	16	18	15	5	12	9	6	8	8	9	8	8	7	10	Dale Earnhardt
4	Bobby Hamilton	37	37	40	40	41	39	41	40	40	39	39	40	40	39	40	39	38	38	Bobby Hamilton
5	Terry Labonte	22	21	23	22	20	17	17	14	13	19	22	20	16	14	13	11	11	11	Terry Labonte
6	Mark Martin	2	2	2	3	1	2	2	2	2	3	3	3	3	3	3	2	4	4	Mark Martin
7	Michael Waltrip	5	5	15	19	19	24	26	27	24	20	24	23	22	23	23	23	24	27	Michael Waltrip
9	Jerry Nadeau	28	29	36	38	38	37	35	32	33	29	29	30	29	32	29	27	32	31	Jerry Nadeau
10	Ricky Rudd	14	13	14	13	12	15	16	17	19	17	17	14	12	12	12	12	10	9	Ricky Rudd
12	Jeremy Mayfield	19	19	16	15	14	11	11	12	15	12	12	13	31	30	28	28	31	29	Jeremy Mayfield
16	Kevin LePage	43	40	38	33	32	30	28	28	31	30	32	29	27	27	26	25	29	30	Kevin LePage
18	Bobby Labonte	7	6	4	4	3	3	3	3	3	2	2	2	2	2	2	4	3	2	Bobby Labonte
20	Tony Stewart	11	11	7	6	5	6	6	6	7	5	8	7	7	7	7	6	8	7	Tony Stewart
21	Elliott Sadler	13	17	20	18	18	20	20	20	22	25	25	24	21	21	18	18	17	21	Elliott Sadler
22	Ward Burton	12	12	10	10	10	8	8	7	9	6	5	5	6	5	6	7	2	6	Ward Burton
23	Jimmy Spencer	42	42	39	36	35	43	39	38	38	37	36	35	34	35	32	32	26	26	Jimmy Spencer
24	Jeff Gordon	1	1	4	1	4	4	4	5	5	4	4	4	4	4	4	5	6	3	Jeff Gordon
25	Wally Dallenbach, Jr.	27	25	24	24	23	21	18	18	16	16	16	17	15	17	15	14	15	14	Wally Dallenbach, Jr.
26	Johnny Benson	39	38	31	29	29	29	23	26	26	21	21	21	20	20	20	19	21	19	Johnny Benson
28	Kenny Irwin	15	16	8	8	8	7	7	8	6	7	10	10	11	16	16	15	19	13	Kenny Irwin

NASCAR season finishing-position grid (car number, driver, finishing positions by race) with race average speeds.

No.	Driver																		
30	Derrike Cope	31	32	41	41	39	36	33	35	35	32	33	31	28	28	30	29	30	32
31	Mike Skinner	6	7	7	9	9	9	10	11	11	15	13	12	14	11	10	10	13	12
33	Ken Schrader	9	9	12	13	14	14	16	18	18	13	14	15	19	18	17	17	16	18
36	Ernie Irvan	40	41	37	36	33	30	30	30	30	26	26	25	23	26	24	24	27	24
40	Sterling Marlin	21	20	20	24	23	25	25	21	18	18	19	19	17	19	16	16	12	16
41	David Green	3	4	9	11	12	13	15	14	29	29	28	27	25	25	21	21	20	20
42	Joe Nemechek	33	31	27	26	32	21	24	32	31	31	28	28	26	29	26	26	22	22
43	John Andretti	10	8	5	7	10	10	9	8	8	8	10	11	10	13	33	33	37	37
44	Kyle Petty	24	26	29	30	35	27	22	23	41	41	41	41	41	41	41	41	41	41
50	Ricky Craven	26	28	28	28	31	36	36	36	33	33	36	38	36	31	35	36	36	34
55	Kenny Wallace	41	43	43	42	41	42	41	41	40	40	39	39	38	40	40	39	39	39
58	Hut Stricklin	36	36	33	31	33	24	23	25	14	15	34	34	39	36	37	34	34	33
60	Geoffrey Bodine	23	22	25	25	28	31	31	27	24	23	22	33	30	10	11	30	25	25
66	Darrell Waltrip	35	33	35	43	40	38	42	42	42	42	42	42	42	42	42	42	42	42
71	Dave Marcis	29	27	32	34	34	34	34	34	34	35	32	30	34	38	38	37	34	40
75	Ted Musgrave	30	30	39	37	42	37	37	37	36	37	36	35	37	37	36	36	35	35
77	Robert Pressley	25	23	21	22	22	22	21	20	23	20	18	18	24	21	20	18	17	17
88	Dale Jarrett	4	3	2	2	1	1	1	1	1	1	1	1	1	1	1	1	1	1
93	Dave Blaney	20	24	27	27	25	29	29	28	35	34	33	32	33	31	31	28	28	28
94	Bill Elliott	8	10	12	14	15	16	33	29	41	27	26	24	22	22	23	23	23	23
97	Chad Little	38	39	37	34	31	27	43	43	27	43	43	43	43	43	43	43	43	43
98	Rick Mast	34	35	42	42	40	38	39	39	38	38	37	37	38	37	34	33	36	36
99	Jeff Burton	16	14	11	9	6	5	4	4	11	7	11	5	5	6	3	5	5	5

Race Average Speed: 163.577, 167.701, 162.884, 148.596, 142.705, 147.188, 149.090, 151.342, 148.228, 168.840, 166.876, 145.191, 150.876, 145.223, 148.742, 150.529, 147.045

DRIVER PROFILES

Those Who Made The Show At The 1999 Brickyard 400

By Al Pearce

Brickyard 400 winners Jeff Gordon, Dale Jarrett, Ricky Rudd, and Dale Earnhardt

The Scoresheet

1994

1st	Jeff Gordon	Hendrick Motorsports Chevrolet
2nd	Brett Bodine	Kenny Bernstein Ford
3rd	Bill Elliott	Junior Johnson Ford

1995

1st	Dale Earnhardt	Richard Childress Racing Chevrolet
2nd	Rusty Wallace	Penske South Racing Ford
3rd	Dale Jarrett	Robert Yates Racing Ford

1996

1st	Dale Jarrett	Robert Yates Racing Ford
2nd	Ernie Irvan	Robert Yates Racing Ford
3rd	Terry Labonte	Hendrick Motorsports Chevrolet

1997

1st	Ricky Rudd	Rudd Performance Motorsports Ford
2nd	Bobby Labonte	Joe Gibbs Racing Pontiac
3rd	Dale Jarrett	Robert Yates Racing Ford

1998

1st	Jeff Gordon	Hendrick Motorsports Chevrolet
2nd	Mark Martin	Roush Racing Ford
3rd	Bobby Labonte	Joe Gibbs Racing Pontiac

1999

1st	Dale Jarrett	Robert Yates Racing Ford
2nd	Bobby Labonte	Joe Gibbs Racing Pontiac
3rd	Jeff Gordon	Hendrick Motorsports Chevrolet

Car Make:
  Ford Taurus
Team Name:
  **Quality Care Service/
  Ford Credit**
Team Owner:
  Robert Yates
Crew Chief:
  Todd Parrott

DALE JARRETT 88

D ale Jarrett emerged in 1999 as the consummate stock car racer and capped his season by winning his first NASCAR title. His runaway victory in the Brickyard 400 left him almost 300 points ahead with 14 races remaining, and that was more than enough for the championship.

Jarrett left no doubt that he was the class of the field this year—just as he might have been if he hadn't run out of gas and lost four laps midway through the 1998 race. His No. 88 Ford led 6 times for a record 117 laps this year and beat Bobby Labonte by a record 3.351 seconds. Jarrett's only brief moment of concern came early when he lightly brushed the Turn 1 wall while checking his mirror. He was virtually unchallenged throughout the second half of the race.

Jarrett is a true son of stock car racing. His father, Ned, was a two-time (1961 and 1965) NASCAR champion who won 50 races before retiring in 1966. Dale's brother, Glenn, raced briefly before following his father into radio and TV. Dale was an outstanding multi-sport high school star before starting in the lower divisions at Hickory, North Carolina, Speedway in the 1970s.

Jarrett ran most of the Busch races (winning 11 of them) between 1982 and 1987 when he got his first real taste of Winston Cup. He ran a season-plus for Cale Yarborough and got his breakthrough victory with the Wood brothers (1990–1991). He drove 3 years for Joe Gibbs before moving to Robert Yates for the 1995 season.

1999 Brickyard 400 Performance Profile

Starting Position	04
Qualifying Average Speed	178.859 mph
Qualifying Speed Rank	04
Finishing Position	01
Laps Completed	160
Laps Led	117
Best Brickyard 400 Finish	01 (1996 & 1999)

**1999 Brickyard 400 Prize Winnings $712,240
Number of Brickyard 400 Appearances 06**

Car Make:
Pontiac Grand Prix
Team Name:
Joe Gibbs Racing
Team Owner:
Joe Gibbs
Crew Chief:
Jimmy Makar

BOBBY LABONTE 18

When Bobby Labonte finished second in the 1999 Brickyard 400, it marked his third consecutive top-5 in the mid-summer race at the Indianapolis Motor Speedway. He was second to Ricky Rudd in 1997, third behind Jeff Gordon and Mark Martin in 1998, then second to Jarrett this year. His other three IMS starts weren't that successful: 16th in the inaugural race in 1994, 9th in 1995, then 24th in 1996.

He was a contender throughout the 1999 event until a mysterious engine skip in his No. 18 Pontiac left him fading in Jarrett's wake over the final laps. Although he led only once for one lap, he doggedly stayed among the front half-dozen throughout the 160-lap, 400-mile race. In fact, after starting 7th, he never was lower than 6th after the first 10-lap scoring report.

Labonte followed older brother Terry into full-time Winston Cup racing in 1993 with team owner Bill Davis. He had prepared for that move by running quarter-midgets and go-karts in Texas, Late Models in North Carolina, and the Busch Series for several years. He was the 1991 Busch Series champion and its 1992 runner-up, and the team owner when David Green won the title in 1994.

After two full Cup seasons with Davis, Labonte replaced Jarrett at Joe Gibbs Racing in 1995. Ironically, his crew chief, Jimmy Makar, is married to Pattie Jarrett, Dale's younger sister. Other than his first victory near Charlotte in 1995, Labonte's brightest memory was winning the 1996 season-finale near Atlanta—on the same day Terry clinched his second championship.

1999 Brickyard 400 Performance Profile

Starting Position	07
Qualifying Average Speed	178.642 mph
Qualifying Speed Rank	07
Finishing Position	02
Laps Completed	160
Laps Led	01
Best Brickyard Finish	02 (1997 & 1999)

1999 Brickyard 400 Prize Winnings $270,950
Number of Brickyard 400 Appearances 06

Car Make:
Chevrolet
Monte Carlo
Team Name:
Hendrick Motorsports
Team Owner:
Rick Hendrick
Crew Chief:
Ray Evernham

JEFF GORDON 24

Jeff Gordon's performance in the 1999 Brickyard 400 only strengthened his well-earned reputation as one of NASCAR's most unyielding drivers. Despite winning the pole and leading 24 of the first 26 laps, his No. 24 Chevrolet never seemed to handle quite well enough to contend for a third IMS victory.

As usual, his crew helped him salvage another top-5 finish. When the last caution waved with 17 laps remaining, most of the drivers ahead of him took either two tires and gas, or no tires at all. But crew chief Ray Evernham and Gordon agreed their car needed four tires, so they sacrificed valuable track position by spending a few more seconds in the pits. After restarting 7th, the three-time champion raced back through traffic for a hard-earned and perhaps surprising 3rd-place finish.

Seldom has anyone had as much impact on any series as Gordon has had on NASCAR. After a brilliant career in USAC open-wheel cars, he shocked almost everyone by choosing stock car racing instead of Indy cars. He was a successful Busch Series driver in the early 1990s for Bill Davis, but bolted to Rick Hendrick and Chevrolet before Davis and Ford Motor Co. could sign him for the 1993 season.

He was the second-youngest champion in NASCAR history and its youngest multiple champion. Fittingly, he made his Winston Cup debut at the Atlanta Motor Speedway in the fall of 1992—the day Richard Petty ran his last race.

1999 Brickyard 400 Performance Profile

Starting Position	01
Qualifying Average Speed	179.612 mph
Qualifying Speed Rank	01
Finishing Position	03
Laps Completed	160
Laps Led	24
Best Brickyard Finish	1st (1994 and 1998)

1999 Brickyard 400 Prize Winnings $262,800
Number of Brickyard 400 Appearances 6

Car Make:
Ford Taurus
Team Name:
Roush Racing
Team Owner:
Jack Roush
Crew Chief:
Jimmy Fennig

MARK MARTIN 06

Nobody will be the least bit surprised when Mark Martin finally wins a Brickyard 400. And make no mistake, he'll get one before he retires. The No. 6 Ford driver has gotten around the Indianapolis Motor Speedway so well for so long that it's only a matter of time until he takes the checkered flag ahead of everybody else. (In something other than an IROC race, that is).

His 4th-place finish in this year's 400 was his fourth top-5 and fifth top-10 in the first six races. His only poor finish was 35th in the inaugural race of 1994. He was 5th the next year, 4th the year after that, then 6th in 1998, 2nd in 1998, and 4th this year. Only Gordon's finishes of 1-6-37-4-1-3 are better than Martin's.

But he lacked just a little something this year. He qualified second to Gordon, then led Laps 6 and 7. He also led Laps 28 through 39 and 64 and 65 before falling back into heavy traffic for the rest of the day. After a late-race caution and restart, Martin ended up edging out Roush Racing teammate Jeff Burton for 4th in the 160-lap, 400-miler.

Martin came to NASCAR after solid ASA and Busch careers. His first stab at Winston Cup in the early 1980s failed, but he returned with owner Jack Roush in 1988 and gradually became one of the tour's most dedicated and successful drivers. Just as a Brickyard 400 victory is in the cards for Martin, so is a Winston Cup.

1999 Brickyard 400 Performance Profile

Starting Position	02
Qualifying Average Speed	178.941 mph
Qualifying Speed Rank	02
Finishing Position	04
Laps Completed	160
Laps Led	16
Best Brickyard 400 Finish	2nd (1998)

1999 Brickyard 400 Prize Winnings $222,450
Number of Brickyard 400 Appearances 6

Car Make:
Ford Taurus
Team Name:
Roush Racing
Team Owner:
Bob Corn
Crew Chief:
Frankie Stoddard

JEFF BURTON 99

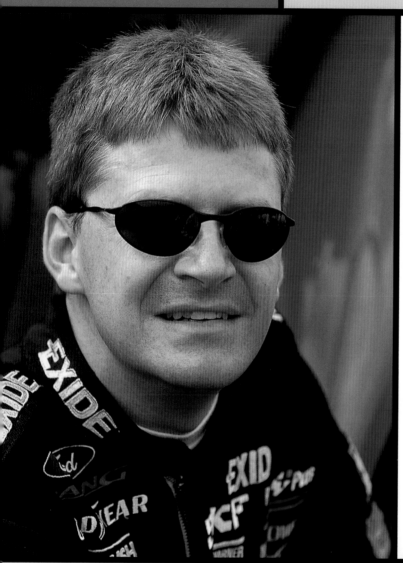

Jeff Burton might have won this year's Brickyard 400 if things had gone a little better in the pits. It seemed that time and time again, either Burton or his crew made a small, almost-imperceptible error that cost him precious seconds on pit road. Even so, his 5th-place finish was by far his best in six Brickyard 400s.

The driver of the No. 99 Ford qualified 16th and managed to lead Lap 117 during an exchange of green-flag pit stops. But the team lost six positions during a yellow-flag stop and had two green-flag stops that weren't as seamless as they generally are. Finally, during the final stop under caution, Burton overruled crew chief Frankie Stoddard by bolting from the pits just as the crew moved to change the left-side tires.

Burton's thinking was that four tires would bring a safe and comfortable top-10, while gambling on 2 to gain track position might just produce an upset victory. In truth, it didn't make much difference: Burton came out of the pits and restarted 5th, and that's where he finished. Whether four tires would have brought him from, say, 7th or 8th to 2nd or 3rd remains one of the day's many unanswered questions.

An excellent short-track career that led to a successful Busch Series career brought Burton to Winston Cup where Jack Roush grabbed him in 1996. Burton comes by his racing interest honestly; he decided to race while watching older brother, Ward, race go-karts in the early 1970s.

1999 Brickyard 400 Performance Profile

Starting Position	16
Qualifying Average Speed	178.038 mph
Qualifying Speed Rank	16
Finishing Position	05
Laps Completed	160
Laps Led	01
Best Brickyard 400 Finish	5th (1998)

1999 Brickyard 400 Prize Winnings $193,240
Number of Brickyard 400 Appearances 6

Car Make:
   Pontiac Grand Prix
Team Name:
   Bill Davis Racing
Team Owner:
   Bill Davis
Crew Chief:
   Tom Baldwin, Jr.

WARD BURTON 22

Ward came from 12th on the grid to as high as 2nd before fading in the final laps. While never a serious contender to win in his No. 22 Pontiac, he nevertheless loitered between 10th and 4th or 5th for most of the afternoon. His gamble on a gas-only pit stop during the last caution paid off for several laps, but when all was said and done, most of the freshly-shod cars easily moved by him.

Like his younger brother, Ward graduated from Virginia go-kart racing in the 1970s to short-track Late Model racing in the 1980s. He had an outstanding Busch career with owner Alan Dillard, and they moved together into Winston Cup in 1994. When financial problems forced the team to fold up late in 1995, Burton joined Bill Davis Racing and quickly got his first Cup victory.

One of the sport's most environmentally conscious drivers, he founded and supports the Ward Burton Wildlife Foundation near his home. Another of his favorite off-track causes is the Patrick Henry School for Boys and Girls.

The Burton brothers of South Boston, Virginia, finished 5th and 6th in this year's Brickyard 400. It matched the best showing by siblings in the 6-year history of the 400-mile NASCAR race at the Indianapolis Motor Speedway. Using a 10-9-8-7-etc. points system, Brett Bodine's 2nd place and brother Todd Bodine's 9th in the 1994 event equals the Burton brothers' 5th and 6th of this year.

1999 Brickyard 400 Performance Profile

Starting Position	12
Qualifying Average Speed	178.324 mph
Qualifying Speed Rank	12
Finishing Position	06
Laps Completed	160
Laps Led	0
Best Brickyard 400 Finish	6th (1999)

1999 Brickyard 400 Prize Winnings $157,210
Number of Brickyard 400 Appearances 6

Car Make:
   Pontiac Grand Prix
Team Name:
   Joe Gibbs Racing
Team Owner:
   Joe Gibbs
Crew Chief:
   Greg Zipadelli

TONY STEWART 20

During a season in which he fared better than anyone might have predicted, Tony Stewart wowed 'em in the Brickyard 400. He started 11th—second-best by a rookie in its 6 runnings—and finished a rookie-record 7th.

The race on Saturday was a blessed relief for the Columbus, Indiana, native. From the moment he arrived home to begin preparing for his first 400, he faced a demanding personal appearance schedule. Friends, family, fans, and the media wanted him. There were speedway and sponsor commitments for Stewart to uphold. Even with a police escort almost everywhere, the local boy making good found it uncommonly difficult to get around.

That's why the race was so refreshing. For the only time that week, Stewart was alone. He quickly brought his No. 20 Pontiac from 11th on the grid to inside the top-10, then stayed there. Except for position changes during green- and yellow-flag pit stops, he stayed between 5th and 8th before taking 7th in the final laps.

The demands on him during the weekend were understandable. More so than Gordon (a Californian by birth) and John Andretti (a Pennsylvanian), Stewart is a true Hoosier. He began in go-karts, then conquered USAC open-wheel racing in the early 1990s. He starred in the Indy Racing League and the Busch Series before joining the Joe Gibbs-owned Winston Cup team for 1999.

His 10th in the Indy 500 and 7th in the Brickyard 400 marked the first time anyone has been top-10 in both Indianapolis Motor Speedway events in the same season.

1999 Brickyard 400 Performance Profile

Starting Position	11
Qualifying Average Speed	178.348 mph
Qualifying Speed Rank	11
Finishing Position	07
Laps Completed	160
Laps Led	0
Best Brickyard 400 Finish	7th (1999) (R)

1999 Brickyard 400 Prize Winnings $162.635
Number of Brickyard 400 Appearances   1

RUSTY WALLACE 02

Car Make:
Ford Taurus
Team Name:
Penske South Racing
Team Owner:
Roger Penske
Crew Chief:
Robin Pemberton

Rusty Wallace has always been among the Brickyard 400's most consistent and successful drivers. He has two top-5s and five top-10s in six starts, and his only downer was an engine-related DNF 38th in 1997. (That was an unusual weekend all around: the potent Roger Penske–owned team took a provisional to start 43rd, then Wallace lasted only 91 laps until his engine blew).

The team's effort this year was significantly better. Wallace qualified only 17th in his No. 2 Ford, then struggled to stay among the high teens for the first 30 of 160 laps. He broke into the top-10 for the first time at Lap 70, then stayed within the top-15 or so until a late-race charge rewarded him with a lead-lap 8th. His team opted for four fresh tires during the final pit stop, a move that briefly dropped him from 9th to 13th in the running order. But he quickly regained all of what he'd lost, plus one more spot when he passed friendly rival Dale Earnhardt in the final laps.

Although the recent years haven't been especially kind to Wallace, he remains one of NASCAR's most popular and competitive drivers. He doesn't win as often as he used to—with Gordon and Jarrett on the prowl, who does?—and hasn't been a serious championship contender since 1993.

Wallace is generally a factor every time the Winston Cup tour visits the Indianapolis Motor Speedway. A guess: if he keeps flirting with Victory Lane, she'll invite him in.

1999 Brickyard 400 Performance Profile

Starting Position	17
Qualifying Average Speed	177.985 mph
Qualifying Speed Rank	17
Finishing Position	08
Laps Completed	160
Laps Led	0
Best Brickyard 400 Finish	2nd (1995)

1999 Brickyard 400 Prize Winnings $140,435
Number of Brickyard 400 Appearances 6

Car Make:
   Ford Taurus
Team Name:
   **Rudd Performance
   Motorsports**
Team Owner:
   Linda Rudd
Crew Chief:
   Mike McSwaim

RICKY RUDD 10

Y ou'd think a NASCAR driver's biggest career victory—and there's no question the 1997 Brickyard 400 was it—would unlock the door to fabulous success and untold riches. For Ricky Rudd, just the opposite was true: his unlikely victory started his self-owned team on a downward spiral that lasted more than two years.

Rudd had only 2 more top-10s in the 13 races following his Indianapolis Motor Speedway victory. He had only 5 top-10s in all of 1998—one of them a late-season victory at Martinsville Speedway. He came into this year's Brickyard 400 without a top-10 in the year's first 19 races, and mired deep into the 30s in points. This, mind you, from a man who's won for 16 consecutive years and was second in the final 1991 standings.

He left Indiana with his best finish of 1999, but it didn't come easy. He had to pass 1995 Brickyard 400 winner Dale Earnhardt on the last lap to move from 10th to 9th. Afterward, an obviously relieved Rudd specified how much of the credit should go to new crew chief Mike McSwaim, with an equal share to Pro Motors. The motors were new to the No. 10 Ford team after less than satisfactory results with motors leased from Penske South.

Rudd's 1975 debut in Winston Cup came shortly after he beat his older brother, Al, in a short-track audition in Virginia. Unlike many of his colleagues, he never ran Saturday night bullrings or struggled in the Busch Series.

1999 Brickyard 400 Performance Profile

Starting Position	14
Qualifying Average Speed	178.130 mph
Qualifying Speed Rank	14
Finishing Position	09
Laps Completed	160
Laps Led	0
Best Brickyard 400 Finish	1st (1997)

1999 Brickyard 400 Prize Winnings $137,535
Number of Brickyard 400 Appearances 6

DALE EARNHARDT 03

Car Make:
Chevrolet Monte Carlo
Team Name:
Richard Childress Racing
Team Owner:
Richard Childress
Crew Chief:
Kevin Hamlin

An unfortunate incident on pit road slowed Rusty Wallace just enough to help Dale Earnhardt win the 1995 Brickyard 400. Well, what goes around comes around, and a minor pit road skirmish in the final laps of this year's race cost The Intimidator a shot at finishing better than 10th.

He wasn't going to win the race; by then, the issue had been long-since settled in Dale Jarrett's favor. But Earnhardt was poised for a possible top-5 finish if he hadn't bumped an errant tire from Jeff Burton's nearby pit with 16 laps remaining. With the left-front of his No. 3 Chevrolet dinged in rather awkwardly, whatever hope Earnhardt had of making a late-race charge was dashed by the aerodynamic mess he had to overcome down the stretch.

The seven-time Winston Cup champion qualified 18th and didn't make much headway in the race's first half. He was no better than 15th during the first 50 laps, then moved into the top-10 near the 80-lap halfway point. Although never a contender to win his second Brickyard 400, Earnhardt nevertheless clung to a top-10 position for the rest of the warm and humid afternoon.

Earnhardt restarted 6th after the last caution, but the caved-in left-front fender held him back. Gordon pushed him to 7th, Rusty Wallace to 8th, Tony Stewart to 9th, then Rudd to 10th on the last lap. Even so, it was his fourth Brickyard top-10 and his fifth lead-lap finish in six starts at the Indianapolis Motor Speedway.

1999 Brickyard 400 Performance Profile

Starting Position	18
Qualifying Average Speed	177.971 mph
Qualifying Speed Rank	18
Finishing Position	10
Laps Completed	160
Laps Led	0
Best Brickyard 400 Finish	1st (1995)

1999 Brickyard 400 Prize Winnings $135,525
Number of Brickyard 400 Appearances 6

Car Make:
Chevrolet Monte Carlo
Team Name:
Hendrick Motorsports
Team Owner:
Rick Hendrick
Crew Chief:
Andy Graves

TERRY LABONTE 05

This year's Brickyard 400 was Terry Labonte's 622nd consecutive Winston Cup start—which is the quietest, most underappreciated record in motorsports. The 1984 and 1996 NASCAR champion broke Richard Petty's record of 513 consecutive starts in April of 1996 and hasn't come close to laying out since. But as with everything else, he doesn't make a big deal out of going to work when you're supposed to.

He started 22nd and finished an uneventful 11th this year at the Indianapolis Motor Speedway. That was almost typical of his other 5 IMS starts: 12th and 13th in the first 2 races, followed by a 3rd in 1996, an engine-related DNF 40th in 1997, then a 9th in 1998. Except for getting barely to the halfway point before blowing up in 1997, Labonte has run all 160 laps in each of his 6 races here.

He stayed between 13th and 23rd for the first half of this year's race. His No. 5 Chevrolet seemed better on long runs, but was a handful in the turns, despite adjustments during pit stops. He was 8th on the last restart, but slipped backward during the frantic 14-lap sprint to the finish, which wasn't nearly enough time for his car to get better as it had during longer runs.

Labonte began racing on Texas short tracks in the early 1970s, then showed his potential with a fourth in his Winston Cup debut—the 1979 Southern 500 at Darlington (Too Tough To Tame) Raceway in South Carolina.

1999 Brickyard 400 Performance Profile

Starting Position	22
Qualifying Average Speed	177.641 mph
Qualifying Speed Rank	22
Finishing Position	11
Laps Completed	160
Laps Led	0
Best Brickyard 400 Finish	3rd (1996)

1999 Brickyard 400 Prize Winnings $129,160
Number of Brickyard 400 Appearances 6

Car Make:
Chevrolet Monte Carlo
Team Name:
Richard Childress Racing
Team Owner:
Richard Childress
Crew Chief:
Larry McReynolds

MIKE SKINNER 31

Very few people remember that Mike Skinner made his Indianapolis Motor Speedway debut in the 1996 Brickyard 400. But you won't find his name listed on the entry list or the final rundown sheet. He came to the speedway strictly in a pinch-hitter role for injured Richard Childress Racing teammate, Dale Earnhardt. A week earlier, Earnhardt had broken a collarbone and his sternum in a horrific crash at the Talladega (Alabama) Superspeedway.

Earnhardt managed to start the Brickyard 400, but yielded to Skinner (still a force in the Craftsman Truck Series at the time), in the early laps. It was an emotional moment for both men: Earnhardt because he was the defending Brickyard 400 champion and Skinner because it reflected the confidence Childress had in him as a Winston Cup driver. That confidence proved well-placed, as Skinner brought the No. 3 Chevrolet home a lead-lap 15th for Earnhardt.

Skinner has run the last three Brickyard 400s in an RCR entry. He was 9th in his rookie season of 1997 and 4th last year, and his 12th this year extended his streak of having run all 160 laps in each of his 4 IMS appearances. After starting 6th, his No. 31 Chevrolet alternated between being loose and tight. He sacrificed track position to take four tires under the last caution (teams that took two tires passed him in the pits), but was mired in so much traffic in the final 14 laps that he couldn't quite get back to the top-10.

1999 Brickyard 400 Performance Profile

Starting Position	06
Qualifying Average Speed	178.667 mph
Qualifying Speed Rank	06
Finishing Position	12
Laps Completed	160
Laps Led	0
Best Brickyard 400 Finish	4th (1998)

1999 Brickyard 400 Prize Winnings $117,010
Number of Brickyard 400 Appearances 3

Car Make:
Ford Taurus
Team Name:
Robert Yates Racing
Team Owner:
Robert Yates
Crew Chief:
Doug Richert

KENNY IRWIN 28

Kenny Irwin was one of four Indiana natives in the sixth-annual Brickyard 400. Not surprisingly, his week was full of public appearances and sponsor commitments. But truth be told, his time at home wasn't nearly as hectic as that of Jeff Gordon and Tony Stewart.

However, Irwin's trip to the Indianapolis Motor Speedway was undoubtedly more stressful in another way. Almost since the third or fourth weekend of the season, talk persisted that his ride in the Robert Yates–owned No. 28 Ford was in jeopardy. For the record, Yates never gave any indication he was displeased with Irwin (who kept saying he was doing all he could do, and that was all he had to say about that).

In his second Brickyard 400, the Indianapolis native qualified 15th and finished a lead-lap 13th. It didn't help Irwin's cause that teammate Dale Jarrett dominated the race and won with a record margin of victory. Irwin ran as high as 6th near the halfway point, but his car lost its handle and dropped back as the race wore on. He managed to stay between 10th and 19th over the final 80 laps before a late-race four-tire stop brought him back to 13th at the finish.

Several days later, the axe fell. What began as a routine weekly meeting ended with Irwin and Yates agreeing it wouldn't serve either's interest to race together for a third year. Well, at least they'll always have Indy.

1999 Brickyard 400 Performance Profile

Starting Position	15
Qualifying Average Speed	178.052 mph
Qualifying Speed Rank	15
Finishing Position	13
Laps Completed	160
Laps Led	0
Best Brickyard 400 Finish	13th (1999)

1999 Brickyard 400 Prize Winnings $111,410
Number of Brickyard 400 Appearances 2

WALLY DALLENBACH JR. 25

Car Make:
Chevrolet Monte Carlo
Team Name:
Hendrick Motorsports
Team Owner:
Rick Hendrick
Crew Chief:
Tony Furr

For someone who grew up with the Indianapolis 500 holding a special place in his heart, Wally Dallenbach Jr., hasn't had much success in the Brickyard 400. In this year's sixth-annual race (his fifth; he didn't race here in 1995), he started 27th and finished a lead-lap 14th, 11 spots behind teammate Jeff Gordon and 3 behind teammate Terry Labonte.

It was a routine and uneventful run—never better than 16th early on, then between 14th and 15th in the final 80 laps. The late-race yellow that allowed teams to refuel and change tires was no friend to Dallenbach and his No. 25 Chevrolet. He was poised to make the finish on the fuel he had and likely would have inherited a top-10 as cars ahead of him began pitting late. Instead, the caution and restart found him mired among lapped traffic for the final 14 laps.

But that's the kind of year it was for the second-generation driver working with his sixth major team since coming to NASCAR in 1991. Several weeks earlier, he'd learned his services wouldn't be needed at Hendrick Motorsports in 2000. It was a bitter pill for the ex-Indy car driver and world-class road racer whose father, Wally Sr., raced in 13 Indy 500s before becoming CART's chief steward.

1999 Brickyard 400 Performance Profile

Starting Position	27
Qualifying Average Speed	177.288 mph
Qualifying Speed Rank	27
Finishing Position	14
Laps Completed	160
Laps Led	0
Best Brickyard 400 Finish	14th (1999)

1999 Brickyard 400 Prize Winnings $109,610
Number of Brickyard 400 Appearances 5

Car Make:
Chevrolet Monte Carlo
Team Name:
Dale Earnhardt Inc.
Team Owner:
Dale and Teresa Earnhardt
Crew Chief:
Paul Andrews

STEVE PARK 01

Who can forget the vicious and frightening way Steve Park exited his inaugural Brickyard 400 in 1998? After overcoming serious early-season leg and hip injuries suffered in a March crash near Atlanta, the rookie was making what seemed like a strong return in the fifth-annual race at the Indianapolis Motor Speedway. Instead, a cut tire between Turns 1 and 2 caused him to crash heavily, without injury, with just 12 laps remaining.

Park's second trip to Indy certainly was safer, but eventful on several fronts. He practiced well, but qualified poorly on the first day, and chose to run the second qualifying session instead of standing on his time. He was fastest in the Friday morning practice and easily made the field by running second-fastest in the last qualifying session. He started the Saturday race from 32nd and steadily came toward the front. He briefly reached 13th in the second half before finishing a lead-lap 15th, 5 spots behind his team owner, Dale Earnhardt.

The late-race caution that helped most drivers did nothing for Park and his No. 1 Chevrolet. Park was better on long green-flag runs than on short, and his car was good to go on the fuel and tires it had. Like Dallenbach just ahead of him, Park likely would have moved into the top-10 if it hadn't been for the late caution that bunched the field.

Despite the disappointment, Park was happy to remind all that this year's 15th finish trounced last year's 35th.

1999 Brickyard 400 Performance Profile

Starting Position	32
Qualifying Average Speed	176.744 mph
Qualifying Speed Rank	32
Finishing Position	15
Laps Completed	160
Laps Led	0
Best Brickyard 400 Finish	15th (1999)

1999 Brickyard 400 Prize Winnings $109,610
Number of Brickyard 400 Appearances 2

Car Make:
Chevrolet Monte Carlo
Team Name:
Team Sabco
Team Owner:
Felix Sabates
Crew Chief:
Scott Eggelston

STERLING MARLIN 40

Competing in his sixth Brickyard 400, Sterling Marlin and his No. 40 Chevrolet team had a mid-pack outing this year at the Indianapolis Motor Speedway. Owner Felix Sabates had a respectable day as both Marlin's car and teammate Joe Nemechek's ran all day without incident. The bad news is that neither car finished very well.

Marlin started 21st, then ranged from a worst of 25th after 50 laps to 12th before slipping back to 16th at the end. Like everyone else, he stopped for tires (in his case, two) and gas when the final yellow waved with 17 laps left. Marlin wasn't able to make any progress when the race restarted for the last time with 14 laps remaining.

The lead-lap finish was Marlin's fourth in his six Brickyard 400s. He was 14th and 7th in the first two, dropped out in 1996 and 1997, was 11th in 1998, then placed 16th this year.

1999 Brickyard 400 Performance Profile

Starting Position	21
Qualifying Average Speed	177.651 mph
Qualifying Speed Rank	21
Finishing Position	16
Laps Completed	160
Laps Led	0
Best Brickyard 400 Finish	7th (1995)

1999 Brickyard 400 Prize Winnings $109,310
Number of Brickyard 400 Appearances 6

Car Make:
Ford Taurus
Team Name:
Jasper Motorsports
Team Owner:
Doug Bawel
Crew Chief:
Charlie Pressley

ROBERT PRESSLEY 77

It was hard to hear at 180 miles per hour, but it's a good bet Robert Pressley let out a huge sigh of relief when he saw the "two-to-go" flags at this year's Brickyard 400. In two of his previous three starts at the Indianapolis Motor Speedway, he crashed out with three laps to go. Thus, his great relief at lap 158 and even greater relief when his No. 77 Ford finished all 160 laps.

It was quite an accomplishment for Pressley. He didn't run the inaugural race in 1994 and didn't have a ride for the 1997 event. He was 28th (2 laps down) in 1995, crashed out with 3 laps remaining in 1996, then crashed out—again, with 3 laps remaining—in 1998. Except for those late-race incidents, Pressley might have finished three of his four Brickyard 400s on the lead lap.

Instead, it wasn't until 1999 that he managed to avoid late-race troubles and finally see the checkered flag—although he was 16 positions behind where he wanted to be. All in all, though, it was a decent day. Pressley started 25th (the last of the first-day qualifiers) and stayed between 25th and 20th for the first 90 laps. He briefly ran 18th, then slipped back to the low 20s until gaining a few spots in the final laps.

His 17th-place finish was only his second lead-lap finish in the year's first 20 races. But if you're looking for a solid payday, the Brickyard 400 is hard to beat.

1999 Brickyard 400 Performance Profile

Starting Position	25
Qualifying Average Speed	177.522 mph
Qualifying Speed Rank	25
Finishing Position	17
Laps Completed	160
Laps Led	0
Best Brickyard 400 Finish	17th (1999)

1999 Brickyard 400 Prize Winnings $100,450
Number of Brickyard 400 Appearances   4

Car Make:
Chevrolet Monte Carlo
Team Name:
Andy Petree Racing
Team Owner:
Andy Petree
Crew Chief:
Sammy Johns

KEN SCHRADER 33

Those marketing and media-relations people working for the company that represents team owner Andy Petree and driver Ken Schrader are clever folks. In the days leading to the sixth-annual Brickyard 400, they were busy handing out small, cutout, cardboard maps of Indiana. Each of them pointed out the 19 dirt tracks, weekend bull-rings, and paved ovals where Schrader has raced sometime or another during his long career.

The Indianapolis Motor Speedway, of course, was among them. But unlike a dozen or so of the 18 other tracks on the map, the 2.5-mile speedway didn't have "Winner" beside it. While Schrader has finished on the lead lap in all six Brickyard 400s—and nobody else can say that; not even the four winners—his best IMS showing has been 7th. That came in the inaugural event, won by then-teammate Jeff Gordon in 1994. Schrader was 19th in 1995, improved to 16th the next year, then climbed to 11th and 10th before slipping back to 18th this year.

This year, Schrader qualified an impressive 9th, then promptly went into a backward free-fall he seemed powerless to stop. He bottomed out at 19th after 110 laps, improved slightly over the next 40 laps, then struggled home 18th among the 21 drivers still on the lead lap. His No. 33 Chevrolet had decent power, but never did handle well enough in the turns to make significant progress through the field. Even so, another lead-lap finish is historic.

1999 Brickyard 400 Performance Profile

Starting Position	9
Qualifying Average Speed	178.518 mph
Qualifying Speed Rank	9
Finishing Position	18
Laps Completed	160
Laps Led	0
Best Brickyard 400 Finish	7th (1994)

1999 Brickyard 400 Prize Winnings $105,410
Number of Brickyard 400 Appearances   6

Car Make:
   Ford Taurus
Team Name:
   Roush Racing
Team Owner:
   Jack Roush
Crew Chief:
   Pat Tryson

JOHNNY BENSON 26

In 1996, as Johnny Benson was headed for Winston Cup rookie of the year honors, he came close to getting an even better trophy. As a rookie, he led 3 times for 70 of the 160 laps in his very first Brickyard 400. That's 31 laps more than anyone else—more, in fact, than winner Dale Jarrett, runner-up Ernie Irvan, and third-place Terry Labonte combined.

Only a series of late-race cautions and pit stops kept the 1995 Busch Series champion from perhaps pulling off a massive upset. Even so, Benson finished 8th that afternoon, then came back for a 7th-place the next year for owner Chuck Rider. He was a lap-down 25th in the 1998 race for owner Jack Roush, and improved slightly with this year's lead-lap 19th.

Benson needed an owner-points provisional to start 39th, then stayed mired in the 30s for the first dozen or so laps. He finally advanced into the mid-20s and stayed there until the final 20 laps when he found a way around David Green to finish 19th.

Benson is part of the five-car Roush Racing stable that includes winners Mark Martin and Jeff Burton, plus fellow teammates Chad Little and Kevin LePage. In this year's 400, Benson was the best of the rest—which was no consolation at all.

1999 Brickyard 400 Performance Profile

Starting Position	39
Qualifying Average Speed	174.686 mph
Qualifying Speed Rank	45
Finishing Position	19
Laps Completed	160
Laps Led	0
Best Brickyard 400 Finish	7th (1997)

1999 Brickyard 400 Prize Winnings $112,410
Number of Brickyard 400 Appearances   4

Car Make:
Chevrolet Monte Carlo
Team Name:
Larry Hedrick Racing
Team Owner:
Larry Hedrick
Crew Chief:
Donnie Disharoon

DAVID GREEN 41

The good news for David Green was that his No. 3 starting spot for the 1999 Brickyard 400 matched the best qualifying effort of his two-plus Winston Cup seasons. Indeed, for a while there he was rubbing elbows with pole-sitter Jeff Gordon and second-fastest Mark Martin. And he was ahead of such luminaries as . . . well, such as everybody else in this year's race. But the bad news was that almost everyone realized one good qualifying lap does not make it a good weekend. If he and his No. 41 Chevrolet could do it for 160 laps, then they'd have something.

Alas, he didn't stay near the front for long. He ran among the top-10 for about 25 laps, then settled in between 11th and 15th for the next 45 laps. He dropped as low as 29th around the halfway point before coming back to 20th in the final handful of laps. His lead-lap 20th-place was better than more than half the drivers in the race. Even more importantly, it was his first lead-lap finish of the season and his best finish of 1999 to date.

This year's 400 at the Indianapolis Motor Speedway was Green's second. In 1997, driving for rookie owner Buz McCall, he started 9th, but lasted only until his engine blew after 137 laps. And while 20th might not seem like much, it was undoubtedly First in Class because Green beat fellow Owensboro, Kentucky, natives Michael and Darrell Waltrip, and Jeremy Mayfield.

Neighborhood bragging rights, indeed.

1999 Brickyard 400 Performance Profile

Starting Position	3
Qualifying Average Speed	178.902 mph
Qualifying Speed Rank	3
Finishing Position	20
Laps Completed	160
Laps Led	0
Best Brickyard 400 Finish	20th (1999)

1999 Brickyard 400 Prize Winnings $101,575
Number of Brickyard 400 Appearances   2

Car Make:
Ford Taurus
Team Name:
Wood Brothers
Team Owner:
Glen Wood
Crew Chief:
Mike Beam

ELLIOTT SADLER 21

In any other year, Elliott Sadler, the ex-Busch series star from Virginia, would have been a viable candidate for Winston Cup rookie of the year. He's good enough on the track, articulate enough off the track, and marketable enough to be considered one of the tour's most solid and dependable first-year drivers. He is, too—if you take Tony Stewart out of the equation. It wouldn't have done any good for Sadler to have waited a year: Dale Earnhardt Jr. and Matt Kenseth will be the top rookies in the 2000 season.

But on the other hand, how many rookies can say they started top-15 and finished top-25 in their Brickyard 400 debut, and finished on the lead lap to boot? (The answer: Johnny Benson in 1996, Mike Skinner in 1997, and Stewart and Sadler this year). Sadler started 13th in his No. 21 Ford, had an up-and-down afternoon at the Indianapolis Motor Speedway, and finally finished 21st, the final driver on the lead lap. After being as low as 25th near halfway, he briefly ran as high as 17th before losing four spots in the frenetic 14-lap sprint following the final caution.

The 24-year-old bachelor is the latest in a long line of full-schedule drivers for the Wood brothers, one of NASCAR's most durable and successful teams. He's hungrier than previous driver Michael Waltrip, leading true believers to feel the Woods will finally snap their 6-year losing streak.

1999 Brickyard 400 Performance Profile

Starting Position	13
Qualifying Average Speed	178.147 mph
Qualifying Speed Rank	13
Finishing Position	21
Laps Completed	160
Laps Led	0
Best Brickyard 400 Finish	21st (1999) (R)

1999 Brickyard 400 Prize Winnings $102,710
Number of Brickyard 400 Appearances 1

Car Make:
Chevrolet Monte Carlo
Team Name:
Team Sabco
Team Owner:
Felix Sabates
Crew Chief:
Tony Glover

JOE NEMECHECK
42

J oe Nemechek was one of a handful of Brickyard 400 drivers to improve significantly from their starting position to their finish position. In this case, "Front-Row Joe'' came forward from 33rd on the 43-car grid to finish 22nd, the first of 11 drivers a lap down at the Indianapolis Motor Speedway. Less than two weeks after the race, he and owner Felix Sabates mutually agreed it would be better if they ended their three-year relationship after the 1999 season.

Nemechek's sixth Brickyard 400 was very similar to his first five, which he ran for three different team owners: once for Larry Hedrick, twice for his self-owned team, and the last three races for Sabates. He qualified as high as 2nd in 1997 and as low as 33rd this year, but finished all six races between 20th and 32nd. Surprisingly, Nemechek ran between 156 and 160 laps in every race, one of the Winston Cup tour's most consistent IMS records.

He was consistent in this year's race, too: after starting 33rd, he raced between there and 21st for the first 80 laps. He slipped as far back as 31st in the second 80 laps before coming back to 22nd in the final laps. It was one of those "I was out there, sort of riding around" types of runs hardly anyone seems to notice.

1999 Brickyard 400 Performance Profile

Starting Position	33
Qualifying Average Speed	176.574 mph
Qualifying Speed Rank	33
Finishing Position	22
Laps Completed	159
Laps Led	0
Best Brickyard 400 Finish	20th (1994)

1999 Brickyard 400 Prize Winnings $100,710
Number of Brickyard 400 Appearances 6

Car Make:
Ford Taurus
Team Name:
Elliott Motorsports
Team Owner:
Bill Elliott
Crew Chief:
Wayne Orme

BILL ELLIOTT 94

For the first time in six Brickyard 400s, former Winston Cup champion Bill Elliott and the No. 94 Ford were pretty much gonzo in this year's race at the Indianapolis Motor Speedway.

NASCAR's all-time favorite driver qualified a solid 8th. That was in keeping with his first three IMS starts of 6th, 4th, and 7th, and certainly better than the 15th and 37th of recent years. But after two top-5s, two top-10s, and a 12th in the first five races here, Elliott struggled to finish 23rd, and was a lap down for the first time. But compared to where he was at times during the afternoon (note that 41st at the halfway point), finishing 23rd didn't look all that bad.

Until this year, Elliott and Ken Schrader were the only drivers to have completed all 800 laps spread among the first five races. Based on a points system giving 10 for first, 9 for second, 8 for third, etc., Elliott ranks right up there with two-time winners Jeff Gordon and Dale Jarrett, and with the ever-consistent Mark Martin as the Speedway's best NASCAR drivers.

1999 Brickyard 400 Performance Profile

Starting Position	08
Qualifying Average Speed	178.547 mph
Qualifying Speed Rank	08
Finishing Position	23
Laps Completed	159
Laps Led	0
Best Brickyard 400 Finish	3rd (1994)

1999 Brickyard 400 Prize Winnings $99,610
Number of Brickyard 400 Appearances 6

Car Make:
Pontiac Grand Prix
Team Name:
MB2 Motorsports
Team Owner:
Nelson Bowers
Crew Chief:
Ryan Pemberton

ERNIE IRVAN 36

E rnie Irvan is the first to admit no speedway owes anybody anything. Pocono Raceway doesn't owe Bobby Allison anything because his career ended there in 1988, just as Talladega Superspeedway doesn't owe Allison anything because his son, Davey, died there in 1993.

On the other hand, if any speedway owes anyone a smooch instead of a slap, the Indianapolis Motor Speedway owes Irvan big-time for his travails in past Brickyard 400s. He was five laps from winning the first one in 1994 when a flat tire left him a lap-down 17th. He missed the 1995 races because of injuries from his 1994 crash at Michigan, then was second to teammate Dale Jarrett in 1996 after slipping in oil while leading at lap 154. Somehow "that's racing" just doesn't seem to cut it.

Irvan won Brickyard 400 poles in 1997 and 1998, and finished a credible 10th and 6th those years. But this year's race was unquestionably the worse of his five here. He needed a provisional to start 40th (by 23 spots, his worst IMS qualifying effort), and his 24th was seven spots worse than his tire-related 17th in 1994.

He was 26th at halfway (his best position to that point) and loitered between 26th and 23rd before finishing 24th. Afterward, he said his No. 36 Pontiac was loose going into the turns and tight coming off. A handful, indeed, for someone who deserves better.

1999 Brickyard 400 Performance Profile

Starting Position	40
Qualifying Average Speed	175.538 mph
Qualifying Speed Rank	40
Finishing Position	24
Laps Completed	159
Laps Led	0
Best Brickyard 400 Finish	2nd (1996)

1999 Brickyard 400 Prize Winnings $98,510
Number of Brickyard 400 Appearances 5

Car Make:
Chevrolet Monte Carlo
Team Name:
Joe Bessey Motorsports
Team Owner:
Joe Bessey
Crew Chief:
Jim Long

GEOFFREY BODINE 60

It's fair to say that Geoffrey Bodine (or, Geoff if you insist on sticking with the pre-1999 pronunciation) has had an inconsistent relationship with the famous Indianapolis Motor Speedway and its mid-summer Brickyard 400.

First, the ups: he qualified 4th for the inaugural race in 1994 and led 24 of the first 95 laps; and he finished on the lead lap in the 1995 and 1997 races, although neither finish (15th and 20th) was especially satisfying. Now, the downs: he crashed out from contact with brother, Brett, after 99 laps in 1994, then made a public spectacle of their family feud; he didn't qualify in 1997; and he finished 37th in 1998 after an accident spoiled his car's handling.

This year's race was neither feast nor famine for the man who was the first driver hired by rookie team-owner Rick Hendrick in 1984. Bodine started 23rd, stayed mostly in the 20s all afternoon, and finished 25th, a lap down in his No. 60 Chevrolet. Because of when pit stops cycled around and when caution flags waved, he was running a heady 10th with 40 laps remaining.

Bodine has 18 career victories (including the 1986 Daytona 500), has won an IROC and Winston all-star championship, and was voted last year among NASCAR's 50 greatest drivers.

1999 Brickyard 400 Performance Profile

Starting Position	23
Qualifying Average Speed	177.627 mph
Qualifying Speed Rank	23
Finishing Position	25
Laps Completed	159
Laps Led	0
Best Brickyard 400 Finish	15th (1995)

1999 Brickyard 400 Prize Winnings $90,710
Number of Brickyard 400 Appearances 5

Car Make:
Ford Taurus
Team Name:
Travis Carter
Motorsports
Team Owner:
Travis Carter
Crew Chief:
Donnie Wingo

JIMMY SPENCER 23

Jimmy Spencer and the Indianapolis Motor Speedway seem alike in some ways. Both are well known for their past successes and present popularity. They're big, charismatic, and don't take any guff from anybody. Spencer is Mr. Excitement and the Speedway is simply The Speedway. Both have a sense that everything is going to be just fine because something better is always just around the corner. Now, if only the driver and the track would learn to get along a little better.

Spencer has run all six Brickyard 400s, but never with a great deal of success. He has qualified twice in the 20s, twice in the 30s, and (counting this year's 42nd) twice in the 40s. His finishes have been equally mediocre: a 12th, 3 finishes in the 20s, 1 in the 30s, and 1 woeful dead-last wreck-related 43rd in the inaugural race of 1994. Despite all those high numbers, the guy says he's in love with the place.

This year's run was nothing to write home about. He took an owner-points provisional to start 42nd, the next-to-last-driver on the grid. He stayed among the last 10 or 12 cars for most of the afternoon, but got into the mid-20s during pit stops for the final caution. His 26th-place finish in his No. 23 Ford was the best he'd run all afternoon.

Mediocre again? Sure, but Spencer can't wait for the 2000 Brickyard 400. He'll get 'em then because for Spencer, something better is always just around the corner.

1999 Brickyard 400 Performance Profile

Starting Position	42
Qualifying Average Speed	176.084 mph
Qualifying Speed Rank	38
Finishing Position	26
Laps Completed	159
Laps Led	0
Best Brickyard 400 Finish	12th (1996)

1999 Brickyard 400 Prize Winnings $96,385
Number of Brickyard 400 Appearances 6

Car Make:
    Chevrolet Monte Carlo
Team Name:
    Mattei Motorsports
Team Owner:
    Jim Mattei
Crew Chief:
    Bobby Kennedy

MICHAEL WALTRIP 07

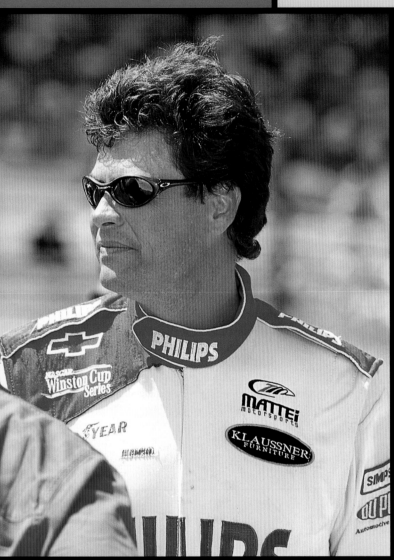

For years, folks around NASCAR haven't quite been able to get a firm handle on Michael Waltrip. He's a great guy, fun to be around, and as personable and media friendly as anyone you'd ever hope to meet. He seems dedicated to racing, and his record of success in Goody's Dash and Busch Series cars indicates he knows what he's doing behind the wheel.

But Waltrip remains a frustrating 0-Fer in his 14-year Winston Cup career. Going into the 1999 Brickyard 400, the younger brother of three-time champion Darrell Waltrip had 414 career starts without once ending in Victory Lane. Michael won the 1996 Winston Select, but that sprint race among a small field of drivers at the Lowe's Charlotte Motor Speedway isn't considered an official points victory.

Waltrip has a handful of Cup top-5s and larger handfuls of career top-10s, but nothing even remotely resembling a victory. And despite a superb 5th-place qualifying in his No. 7 Chevrolet, he didn't come close to getting it in the latest Brickyard 400. After 160 laps around the Indianapolis Motor Speedway, he was 27th, the 6th of 11 drivers a lap down. It took only 10 laps for him to lose the top-10 and only 30 laps for him to fall into the top-20.

1999 Brickyard 400 Performance Profile

Starting Position	05
Qualifying Average Speed	178.816 mph
Qualifying Speed Rank	05
Finishing Position	27
Laps Completed	159
Laps Led	0
Best Brickyard 400 Finish	8th (1994)

1999 Brickyard 400 Prize Winnings $94,885
Number of Brickyard 400 Appearances 6

Car Make:
Pontiac Grand Prix
Team Name:
Bill Davis Racing
Team Owner:
Bill Davis
Crew Chief:
Gil Martin

DAVE BLANEY 93

When Dave Blaney left the relative comfort of the World of Outlaws to try NASCAR, he probably figured it would be 2000 before his Brickyard 400 debut. That's because team owner Bill Davis and sponsor Amoco wanted him to run two seasons of the Busch Series before trying Winston Cup with teammate Ward Burton. But there Blaney was, qualifying a credible 20th and finishing a lap-down 28th in the 1999 race at the Indianapolis Motor Speedway. While it certainly was a memorable day, it was far from successful. The 1996 Sprint Car champion was 35th at halfway and managed to reach 28th with good pit strategy near the finish. But when he and Davis look back on their 1999 effort at Indy, they'll feel good about making the field (a handful of "name" drivers didn't) and bringing their No. 93 Pontiac home unscathed.

Blaney is the latest Sprint Car driver—but not the most well-known—to turn to stock car racing. Brad Noffsinger and Sammy Swindell tried it in the late 1980s with little success. Former Cup owner Kenny Bernstein went out on a limb by hiring outlaw legend Steve Kinser for the 1995 season—an experiment that lasted about a third of the season.

If form holds, Blaney will be just fine. His Busch experience and five Cup races this year will serve him well in 2000.

1999 Brickyard 400 Performance Profile

Starting Position	20
Qualifying Average Speed	177.708 mph
Qualifying Speed Rank	20
Finishing Position	28
Laps Completed	159
Laps Led	0
Best Brickyard Finish	28th (1999) (R)

1999 Brickyard 400 Prize Winnings $84,385
Number of Brickyard 400 Appearances 1

Car Make:
Ford Taurus
Team Name:
Kranefuss-Penske Racing
Team Owner:
Michael Kranefuss
Crew Chief:
Peter Sospenzo

JEREMY MAYFIELD 12

When Jeremy Mayfield got his breakthrough Winston Cup victory at the Pocono (Pennsylvania) Raceway in the summer of 1998, some NASCAR-watchers hailed it as the first of many. Everybody said the kid is good, and with a crew chief like Peter Sospenzo and owners like veterans Michael Kranefuss and Roger Penske, the sky is the limit.

Actually, that 500-mile Pocono victory is beginning to look more and more like a fluke. Mayfield's well-sponsored and highly-visible No. 12 Ford hasn't won since Pocono, and mid-pack finishes and personnel changes suggest that all isn't well on the North Carolina-based team.

Mayfield's 29th-place finish in the sixth-annual Brickyard 400 can be blamed more on a faulty transmission than anything he or his crew did. After qualifying 19th in the first session at the Indianapolis Motor Speedway, he was running a solid 12th at the halfway point on Saturday. He seemed capable of perhaps getting a top-10 to go with his impressive 5th-place finish of two years ago. All good thoughts vanished when Mayfield lost second gear at halfway, and then third gear not long after.

Given all that, it's remarkable he managed to finish within a lap of the winner. Mayfield now has four Brickyard 400 finishes in the 20s, the giddy 5th-place finish of 1997, and last year's forgettable 42nd.

1999 Brickyard 400 Performance Profile

Starting Position	19
Qualifying Average Speed	177.925 mph
Qualifying Speed Rank	19
Finishing Position	29
Laps Completed	159
Laps Led	0
Best Brickyard 400 Finish	5th (1997)

1999 Brickyard 400 Prize Winnings $98,885
Number of Brickyard 400 Appearances 6

Car Make:
Ford Taurus
Team Name:
Roush Racing
Team Owner:
Jack Roush
Crew Chief:
Skip Eyler

KEVIN LEPAGE 16

Kevin LePage earned his spot on the starting grid the hard way. He broke into Busch series racing by campaigning a self-owned team and running without a major sponsor in 1996. His success under trying circumstances brought him a better Busch ride. He moved to Winston Cup competition in 1998 with a Joe Falk-owned car, also without a major sponsor. Finishing respectably in the Winston Cup without a major sponsor is not an easy feat, but LePage pulled it off with enough decent finishes to attract the attention of Roush Racing, putting LePage behind the wheel of one of Jack Roush's cars for the 1999 season.

Unfortunately, that ride only brought LePage a mediocre weekend on the bricks. He took a provisional to start last on the 43-car grid, then stayed mired in the 30s and 40s for most of the race. He cracked the top-20 for some of the second half, but dropped from 25th to 30th over the final 20 laps. Granted it was his first start at IMS, but it also was the first for Tony Stewart (7th), Elliott Sadler (21st), and Dave Blaney (28th).

1999 Brickyard 400 Performance Profile

Starting Position	43
Qualifying Average Speed	175.125 mph
Qualifying Speed Rank	44
Finishing Position	30
Laps Completed	159
Laps Led	0
Best Brickyard 400 Finish	30th (1999) (R)

1999 Brickyard 400 Prize Winnings $90,910
Number of Brickyard 400 Appearances 1

Car Make:
Ford Taurus
Team Name:
Melling Racing
Team Owner:
Mark Melling
Crew Chief:
Newt Moore

JERRY NADEAU 09

In some ways, Jerry Nadeau's second Brickyard 400 was strikingly similar to his first in 1998. That year, he arrived at the Indianapolis Motor Speedway shortly after a minor career change from the ill-fated Bill Elliott/Dan Marino–owned No. 13 Ford team to the rock-solid No. 9 Ford team owned by NASCAR fixture Harry Melling. Last year, Nadeau needed a provisional to start 42nd on the 43-car grid and finished a disappointing lap-down 26th after a quiet and largely uneventful run.

He came to the Speedway for this year's race shortly after learning of a major career change. In 2000, the one-time sports car star will move from the No. 9 Ford to the No. 25 Hendrick Motorsports Chevrolet.

But that's next year. This year's Brickyard 400 was with the Melling team, plugging on despite the death of team founder/owner Harry Melling in May. Wishing for so much better, Nadeau qualified 28th and finished a lap-down 31st. Simply put, it was an unremarkable run by a driver who would give almost anything to strap himself into a Formula One car for the United States Grand Prix in September of 2000 around the Speedway's new infield road course.

1999 Brickyard 400 Performance Profile

Starting Position	28
Qualifying Average Speed	177.144 mph
Qualifying Speed Rank	28
Finishing Position	31
Laps Completed	159
Laps Led	0
Best Brickyard 400 Finish	26th (1998)

1999 Brickyard 400 Prize Winnings $83,485
Number of Brickyard 400 Appearances 2

Car Make:
Pontiac Grand Prix
Team Name:
Bahari/Eel River Racing
Team Owner:
Jack Birmingham
Crew Chief:
Barry Dodson

DERRIKE COPE 30

A season lacking any meaningful highlights for Derrike Cope finally produced some optimism in the days before the Brickyard 400. After years as the primary owner of Bahari Racing, Chuck Rider sold part of his No. 30 Pontiac team to Jack Birmingham. Rider's new partner is a wealthy, well-connected, Boston-based lawyer and businessman who spends much of his time in Florida. Hardly anyone who knows Birmingham doubts he'll be a success at racing.

The team's first hire was a good one. Former championship (with Rusty Wallace) crew chief Barry Dodson came aboard in time for the August 1 race at the Indianapolis Motor Speedway. Working with little knowledge of his equipment and makeshift crew, Dodson helped qualify Cope in 31st. The team finished one position worse than that, but was only one lap down to winner Dale Jarrett.

If you're wondering how that can be called optimistic, consider this: before Dodson and fellow newcomer Buddy Barnes signed on, only 8 of Cope's 19 previous qualifying efforts had earned him a spot on the grid. He had missed nine events (including three in a row) and had needed provisionals to start two other races. His Brickyard 400 run was thoroughly mediocre: he ranged between 28th and 42nd due to an engine skip and a balky chassis.

1999 Brickyard 400 Performance Profile

Starting Position	31
Qualifying Average Speed	176.835 mph
Qualifying Speed Rank	31
Finishing Position	32
Laps Completed	159
Laps Led	0
Best Brickyard 400 Finish	14th (1996)

1999 Brickyard 400 Prize Winnings $82,385
Number of Brickyard 400 Appearances 5

Car Make:
Ford Taurus
Team Name:
Scott Barbour III
Team Owner:
SB III Motorsports
Crew Chief:
Mike Hillman

HUT STRICKLIN 58

Hut Stricklin has a lot going for him. He came up through the Winston Racing Series bullrings and Goody's Dash ranks, and has driven with occasional distinction for some fairly well-known owners—Junior Johnson, Ron Osterlund, Bobby Allison, Kenny Bernstein, Travis Carter, the Stavola brothers, Junie Donlavey, and Scott Barbour. Couple that with the fact that he's married to an Allison (Pam, daughter of Donnie and niece of Bobby), Stricklin knows a lot of the right people. Despite this, his career has been less than a cake walk.

Stricklin's 1999 appearance at IMS marked his fourth start. With each appearance, he has raced for different owners: Carter in 1994, Bernstein in 1995, the Stavolas in 1996, and in Barbour's No. 58 Ford this year. He qualified 36th and was the last driver to make the field via speed. Stricklin finished 33rd, two laps down. He was briefly scored among the top-15 around halfway, but that was primarily the result of pit stops and cautions. Sadly for many midpack to backmarkers, it was the kind of run only close friends and family, or sponsors or potential sponsors, ever notice.

1999 Brickyard 400 Performance Profile

Starting Position	36
Qualifying Average Speed	176.433 mph
Qualifying Speed Rank	36
Finishing Position	33
Laps Completed	158
Laps Led	0
Best Brickyard 400 Finish	18th (1996)

1999 Brickyard 400 Prize Winnings $82,135
Number of Brickyard 400 Appearances 4

Car Make:
   Chevrolet Monte Carlo
Team Name:
   Midwest Transit
   Motorsports
Team Owner:
   Hal Hicks
Crew Chief:
   John Monson

RICKY CRAVEN 50

Once considered among NASCAR's most promising young drivers, Ricky Craven's star-crossed career has seen more twists and turns than Tennessee blacktop. There is nothing to indicate it'll turn into an interstate for Craven anytime soon.

He came to this year's Brickyard 400 after losing his ride with rookie owner Scott Barbour III. Racing's odd couple—Craven is from Maine, Barbour from Florida—began 1999 with high hopes and shaky sponsorship. They made 11 of the first 12 races—missing only at Charlotte—before agreeing they'd be better off working with others. Barbour hired Loy Allen and Craven replaced Dan Pardus in the No. 50 Chevrolet.

Craven and his new team qualified 26th on the first day of time trials and wisely stood on their time. Just making the field was a major victory, never mind that Craven spent all of Saturday's race wallowing in the 20s and 30s. He finished two laps down, but the team's $81,885 payday was its best of the season.

Craven has had a strange ride. From local short-track star to Busch North champion, and then to Winston Cup rookie of the year en route to a dream deal with Hendrick Motorsports. But he had some spectacular crashes, seemed fragile, and quit Hendrick Motorsports in 1998, citing the effects of post-concussion syndrome.

1999 Brickyard 400 Performance Profile

Starting Position	26
Qualifying Average Speed	177.459 mph
Qualifying Speed Rank	26
Finishing Position	34
Laps Completed	158
Laps Led	0
Best Brickyard 400 Finish	16th (1997)

1999 Brickyard 400 Prize Winnings $81,885
Number of Brickyard 400 Appearances 5

Car Make:
Ford Taurus
Team Name:
Butch Mock
Motorsports
Team Owner:
Butch Mock
Crew Chief:
Jon Wolfe

TED MUSGRAVE 75

O n the Friday morning before the Brickyard 400, driver Ted Musgrave and team owner Butch Mock met with the motorsports media in a conference room adjacent to Gasoline Alley at the Indianapolis Motor Speedway. Joining them at the head table was Tennessee media and advertising magnate Darwin Oordt, the No. 75 Ford team's new business partner. Not surprisingly, the mood was positive and upbeat since Oordt said he was there to free Mock of all business and sponsorship worries.

Musgrave had reason to smile, too. After running slower than expected in Thursday's first qualifying session, he was much faster in the Friday practice session. Not long after the press conference, he went out and became the fastest second-round qualifier. That was good enough for 30th on the 43-car grid, behind four drivers who had stood on their time.

The 160-lap, 400-mile race itself wasn't quite so rewarding: Musgrave fought a stubborn push throughout the afternoon and came home 35th, 3rd among the 5 drivers 2 laps down. After lead-lap finishes of 13th, 16th, and 21st in the first 3 Brickyard 400s (followed by a 33rd, then a lead-lap 19th last year), this year's finish was the worst of his 6 IMS appearances.

It was the car's third or fourth time out (Musgrave wasn't exactly sure), and it had driven like a crooked tractor each time. Nothing the team did on Thursday, Friday, or Saturday improved matters appreciably, so Musgrave hinted that the car was not long for this world. He said something about looking for a cutting torch.

1999 Brickyard 400 Performance Profile

Starting Position	30
Qualifying Average Speed	176.946 mph
Qualifying Speed Rank	30
Finishing Position	35
Laps Completed	158
Laps Led	0
Best Brickyard 400 Finish	13th (1994)

1999 Brickyard 400 Prize Winnings $84,110
Number of Brickyard 400 Appearances   6

Car Make:
Ford Taurus
Team Name:
**Cale Yarborough
Motorsports**
Team Owner:
Cale Yarborough
Crew Chief:
Mark Tutor

RICK MAST 98

Remember how Rick Mast was the star of qualifying for the inaugural Brickyard 400? How he stunned everyone by winning the pole, then delighted them with the tale of trading his prized cow for a dirt-track car all those years ago in the Blue Ridge Mountains? And then he went out and led the first two laps of the Speedway's first Winston Cup race before finishing 22nd, a lap behind winner Jeff Gordon. Nobody resented him for all the attention because Mast was, and continues to be, one of NASCAR's good guys.

That's good, because with a sponsor like Woody Woodpecker riding atop one of NASCAR's more creative paint jobs, he needs all the patience and humor he can muster. He also needs it to field the endless string of questions about the ownership and sponsorship situation surrounding the Cale Yarborough–owned No. 98 Ford team he joined in 1999.

Mast's performance in the 1999 race at the Indianapolis Motor Speedway was by far the worst in his six runs here. He started 34th, then loitered between 33rd and 42nd before finishing 36th, 2 laps behind winner Dale Jarrett. His previous Brickyard 400 finishes with owner Richard Jackson were 22nd, 8th, and 9th, then 23rd and 22nd with Butch Mock. All but the first were lead-lap finishes.

1999 Brickyard 400 Performance Profile

Starting Position	34
Qualifying Average Speed	176.512 mph
Qualifying Speed Rank	34
Finishing Position	36
Laps Completed	158
Laps Led	0
Best Brickyard 400 Finish	8th (1995)

1999 Brickyard 400 Prize Winnings $81,510
Number of Brickyard 400 Appearances 6

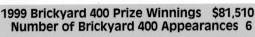

JOHN ANDRETTI 43

Car Make:
Pontiac Grand Prix
Team Name:
Petty Enterprises
Team Owner:
Richard Petty
Crew Chief:
Robbie Loomis

John Andretti spent his formative years in Indianapolis and still calls it home. For the record, he was born in Bethlehem, Pennsylvania, and lives near Charlotte, North Carolina. He grew up near the Indianapolis Motor Speedway and could hear cars testing as he fidgeted at nearby Cardinal Ritter High School.

Aldo's son, Mario's nephew, and Michael's cousin had run several Indy 500s when NASCAR ran its first Brickyard 400 in 1994. Earlier that year, Andretti had become the first man to run the 500 and the Coca-Cola 600 Winston Cup race at the Charlotte Motor Speedway on the same day. So perhaps more than anyone—certainly equal to Kenny Irwin, another Indianapolis native—Andretti longs to do well here.

In truth, his 1999 appearance wasn't as bad as it looks. He practiced well, qualified 10th, and practiced well in the final two sessions. He spent much of Saturday in the top-10, and occasionally got his No. 43 Pontiac into the top-5. But a series of nagging problems with his car's wheels and lugnuts required green-flag stops that cost him two laps and any hope for a top-5. His 37th-place, the last of 5 drivers 2 laps down, was a bummer after being on the lead lap and top-10 after 110 of 160 laps.

To cap his disappointing day, the only damage to Andretti's car was an inadvertent ramming from Jeremy Mayfield after the race in the garage area. Strange, some would say, but it wasn't on this day.

1999 Brickyard 400 Performance Profile

Starting Position	10
Qualifying Average Speed	178.476 mph
Qualifying Speed Rank	10
Finishing Position	37
Laps Completed	158
Laps Led	0
Best Brickyard 400 Finish	7th (1998)

1999 Brickyard 400 Prize Winnings $96,410
Number of Brickyard 400 Appearances 6

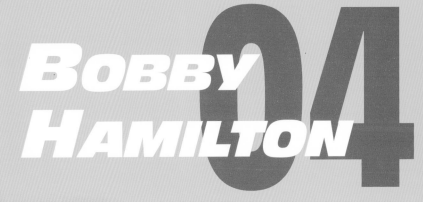

BOBBY HAMILTON 04

Car Make:
Chevrolet Monte Carlo
Team Name:
Morgan-McClure
Motorsports
Team Owner:
Larry McClure
Crew Chief:
Steve Gray

If they had given a bonus for consistency in the Brickyard 400, it likely would have gone to Bobby Hamilton. He started 37th; the first driver in line when provisionals were distributed after the fastest 36 drivers went in by qualifying. On race day, Hamilton was scored no better than 37th and no worse than 40th for the entire race. He finished 38th, the first driver three laps behind.

Unfortunately, that has been typical of his Winston Cup starts at the Indianapolis Motor Speedway. Hamilton was a lap-down 24th in the 1994 opener for owner Felix Sabates. He was a lead-lap 11th the next year and 31st in 1996 before a lead-lap 20th, both for Petty Enterprises. His last two starts with the Morgan-McClure team produced a lead-lap 20th and this year's three-down 38th.

Hamilton got into Winston Cup after working with the producers of the film *Days of Thunder* in 1989. His role as a driver/consultant and his impressive short-track resume led to a Rookie of the Year–winning ride with George Bradshaw in 1991. He ran 1992 for Bradshaw before driving for several owners in 1993.

But his career gained stability when Sabates hired him for 1994. That led to three years in Petty's famous No. 43, where Hamilton got his first (Phoenix, October 1996) and second (Rockingham, Fall 1997) victories. His third came at Martinsville in 1998, giving him a victory per year for the last three years.

1999 Brickyard 400 Performance Profile

Starting Position	37
Qualifying Average Speed	172.381 mph
Qualifying Speed Rank	51
Finishing Position	38
Laps Completed	157
Laps Led	0
Best Brickyard 400 Finish	11th (1995)

1999 Brickyard 400 Prize Winnings $96,310
Number of Brickyard 400 Appearances 6

Car Make:
Chevrolet Monte Carlo
Team Name:
Andy Petree Racing
Team Owner:
Andy Petree
Crew Chief:
Jimmy Elledge

KENNY WALLACE 55

In a way, you have to feel for Kenny Wallace and his No. 55 Chevrolet. They started 41st in the Brickyard 400, ran all but three of the 160 laps, and still finished 39th among the 43 cars. In 13 of the race's 16 scoring periods—each of them at 10-lap intervals—Wallace scored in the 40s.

What's so sad is that nothing extraordinarily bad befell his car. It was a new one: a special version owner Andy Petree and crew chief Jimmy Elledge built specifically for this year's race at the Indianapolis Motor Speedway. They tried to duplicate one of their best flat-track cars, one that had run well at Phoenix and Loudon. But whatever it was that car had, this one didn't.

Wallace wasn't shy about admitting it. He called his team's creation "a special car for a special race . . . and it bit us." Then he acknowledged what was obvious to everyone at the track: "We'll just go on back home with an ol' fashioned butt-whipping from Indianapolis." That kind of self-effacing honesty makes the youngest of the three racing Wallace brothers one of the tour's most popular drivers.

Kenny followed older brother Rusty into Winston Cup after prepping in ASA and Busch races. He won eight times in Busch between 1991 and 1996, which earned a tryout with Robert Yates Racing. His four-year Cup ride with Fil Martocci ended last year, but Wallace ended up just fine—unlike his latest trip to IMS.

1999 Brickyard 400 Performance Profile

Starting Position	41
Qualifying Average Speed	175.128 mph
Qualifying Speed Rank	43
Finishing Position	39
Laps Completed	157
Laps Led	0
Best Brickyard 400 Finish	30th (1997)

1999 Brickyard 400 Prize Winnings $81,210
Number of Brickyard 400 Appearances 5

Car Make:
Chevrolet Monte Carlo
Team Name:
Marcis Auto Racing
Team Owner:
Helen Marcis
Crew Chief:
Bob Marcis

DAVE MARCIS 71

Regardless of how much longer he hangs in Winston Cup racing, long-time driver and all-time gentleman Dave Marcis will look back on the 1999 Brickyard 400 with a smile. Not only did the 57-year-old qualify 29th, but he became the event's all-time oldest leader when he stayed out an extra lap during the second caution just so he could lead Lap 75.

Alas, the popular driver of the No. 71 Chevrolet couldn't sustain that position. He was the first of the four drivers listed on the rundown as Did Not Finish. The engine-related problems that ended his run left the five-time career Cup winner 21 laps behind in 40th place. Still, he earned more than $82,000; considerably more than what he earned during the entire 30-race Winston Cup season of 1974—when two-time Brickyard 400 champion Jeff Gordon was just three years old.

This was Marcis' fourth Cup appearance at the Indianapolis Motor Speedway. Marcis was 41st in the 1994 Brickyard, 35th in 1996, then 41st last year. This year marked his 856th career NASCAR start dating to 1968. That's second to the untouchable 1,177 of Richard Petty, but Marcis has bragging rights in one area—Petty retired the year before NASCAR finally went to the Brickyard.

1999 Brickyard 400 Performance Profile

Starting Position	29
Qualifying Average Speed	177.078 mph
Qualifying Speed Rank	29
Finishing Position	40
Laps Completed	139
Laps Led	1
Best Brickyard 400 Finish	35th

1999 Brickyard 400 Prize Winnings	$82,010
Number of Brickyard 400 Appearances	4

Car Make:
Pontiac Grand Prix
Team Name:
Petty Enterprises
Team Owner:
Richard Petty
Crew Chief:
Doug Hewitt

KYLE PETTY 44

Almost regardless of whatever success Kyle Petty enjoys at the Indianapolis Motor Speedway, it'll be hard not to first think of his crash during the 1996 Brickyard 400. A cut tire and broken brake line sent him into the outside wall in Turn 4. Left with no escape route, Sterling Marlin plowed into Petty and shoved him back into the wall. The battered car ended up slamming into the inside wall near the pit road opening.

Until this year, that was the No. 44 Pontiac driver's only real disagreement with IMS. He ran all but one lap in each of the first two Brickyard 400s—finishing 25th both years for Felix Sabates—then crashed out. After moving to Petty Enterprises in 1997, he had lead-lap finishes of 13th and 14th. Now, it can be said, he's crashed at both ends of the massive 2.5-mile speedway.

Just as in 1996, a cut tire and inability to steer or stop sent Petty into the Turn 1 wall at Lap 74. He started 24th—one of the lucky first-day qualifiers—and stayed in the mid-20s and low-30s until crashing at Lap 74. The nose of his car was bashed in and there was a brief oil fire, but nothing serious. Petty needed some steadying once he got out of the car, but he was not injured.

Photos of him sprawled out and gasping for breath made all the papers, very similar to 1996. As usual, he took it well. The only thing hurt, he said, were his feelings.

1999 Brickyard 400 Performance Profile

Starting Position	24
Qualifying Average Speed	177.546 mph
Qualifying Speed Rank	24
Finishing Position	41
Laps Completed	72
Laps Led	0
Best Brickyard 400 Finish	13th (1997)

1999 Brickyard 400 Prize Winnings $81,010
Number of Brickyard 400 Appearances 6

Car Make:
Ford Taurus
Team Name:
Travis Carter
Motorsports
Team Owner:
Travis Carter/Carl Haas
Crew Chief:
Philippe Lopez

DARRELL WALTRIP 66

This year's Brickyard 400 weekend began with an announcement that confirmed one of NASCAR's worst-kept secrets. On Thursday morning before qualifying, three-time (1981, 1982, 1985) Winston Cup champion Darrell Waltrip hosted a breakfast for the media and Kmart executives. To the surprise of absolutely nobody, he said next year would wrap up his Winston Cup career and his "Victory Tour 2000" would begin with the Daytona 500.

Looking back, he said, it had been a pretty good ride: 3 titles, 59 poles, 85 victories, 2 Most Popular Driver awards, and almost $18 million in earnings since his modest debut in 1972. He came into this year's race at the Indianapolis Motor Speedway burdened with a 213-race losing streak dating to September 1992; he'd been top-10 in only a few dozen races since that victory.

Waltrip's latest Brickyard 400 mirrored that skid. Out of provisionals, he gambled by standing on his first-day qualifying rank of 32nd. Three second-round drivers bumped him down the ladder, but he still made his sixth Brickyard 400 field in 35th. His day ended when his No. 66 Ford developed an engine problem and retired after 58 mediocre laps.

1999 Brickyard 400 Performance Profile

Starting Position	35
Qualifying Average Speed	176.478 mph
Qualifying Speed Rank	35
Finishing Position	42
Laps Completed	58
Laps Led	0
Best Brickyard 400 Finish	6th (1994)

1999 Brickyard 400 Prize Winnings $80,910
Number of Brickyard 400 Appearances 6

Car Make:
Ford Taurus
Team Name:
Roush Racing
Team Owner:
Jack Roush
Crew Chief:
Jeff Hammond

CHAD LITTLE 97

Chad Little's most memorable line during the 1999 race came when he referred to Geoffrey Bodine as a "bald-headed cue ball," The apt description—after all, Bodine is undeniably lacking in head cover—came after Bodine was part of the early-race accident that sent Little into the Turn 2 wall and brought the first of the day's three caution flags at the Indianapolis Motor Speedway.

When asked about the accident, the uninjured, but seriously unhappy, Little voiced his opinion of Bodine. Moments later, perhaps realizing his every word and thought were being chronicled for dispatch around the world, he decided to step back and hold his tongue. But he was right—TV replays clearly show Bodine getting into the back of Little's No. 97 Ford not once, but twice going into Turn 1 at Lap 41. Once the second contact was made, Little was just along for the ride.

It was an altogether fitting end to a bad weekend for the Washington State and Gonzaga graduate. He took a provisional to start 38th, joining fellow Roush Racing drivers Kevin LePage and Johnny Benson near the back of the Winston Cup grid. (Roush teammates Mark Martin started 2nd and Jeff Burton 16th). Little had come up to 27th when his race ended with a bang . . . as it did in the 1997 and 1998 Brickyard 400s.

Three starts. Three poor qualifying efforts. Three crashes.

1999 Brickyard 400 Performance Profile

Starting Position	38
Qualifying Average Speed	175.254 mph
Qualifying Speed Rank	42
Finishing Position	43
Laps Completed	41
Laps Led	0
Best Brickyard 400 Finish	28th (1997)

1999 Brickyard 400 Prize Winnings $91,605
Number of Brickyard 400 Appearances 3

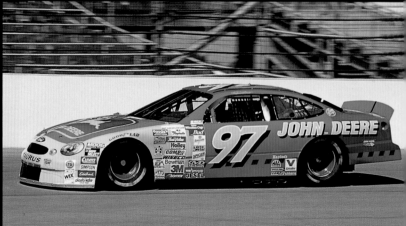